FROM THE
LIBRARY OF

TERRI
TOWER

PICNICS

MARILYN MYERS

PICNICS

MARILYN MYERS

A RUNNING PRESS/FRIEDMAN GROUP BOOK

RUNNING PRESS
PHILADELPHIA, PENNSYLVANIA

A RUNNING PRESS/FRIEDMAN GROUP BOOK

Copyright © 1988 by Michael Friedman Publishing Group, Inc.

9   8   7   6   5   4   3   2   1

Digit on the right indicates the number of this printing.

Library of Congress Cataloging-in-Publication Number: 87-42998

ISBN 0-89471-583-6

PICNICS
was prepared and produced by
Michael Friedman Publishing Group, Inc.
15 West 26th Street
New York, New York 10010

Editor: Nancy Kalish
Photo Editor: Philip Hawthorne
Editorial Assistant: Sharon Kalman
Art Director: Mary Moriarty
Designer: Liz Trovato
Production Manager: Karen L. Greenberg

Typeset by I, CLAVDIA Inc.
Color separations by Hong Kong Scanner Craft Company Ltd.
Printed and bound in Hong Kong by Leefung-Asco Printers Ltd.

This book may be ordered from the Publisher.
Please include $1.50 postage.
But try your bookstore first.

Running Press Book Publishers
125 South Twenty-second Street
Philadelphia, Pennsylvania 19103

DEDICATION

To Agnes Myers and Sally Manesberg Flanzer.
With special thanks to Jim Roper.

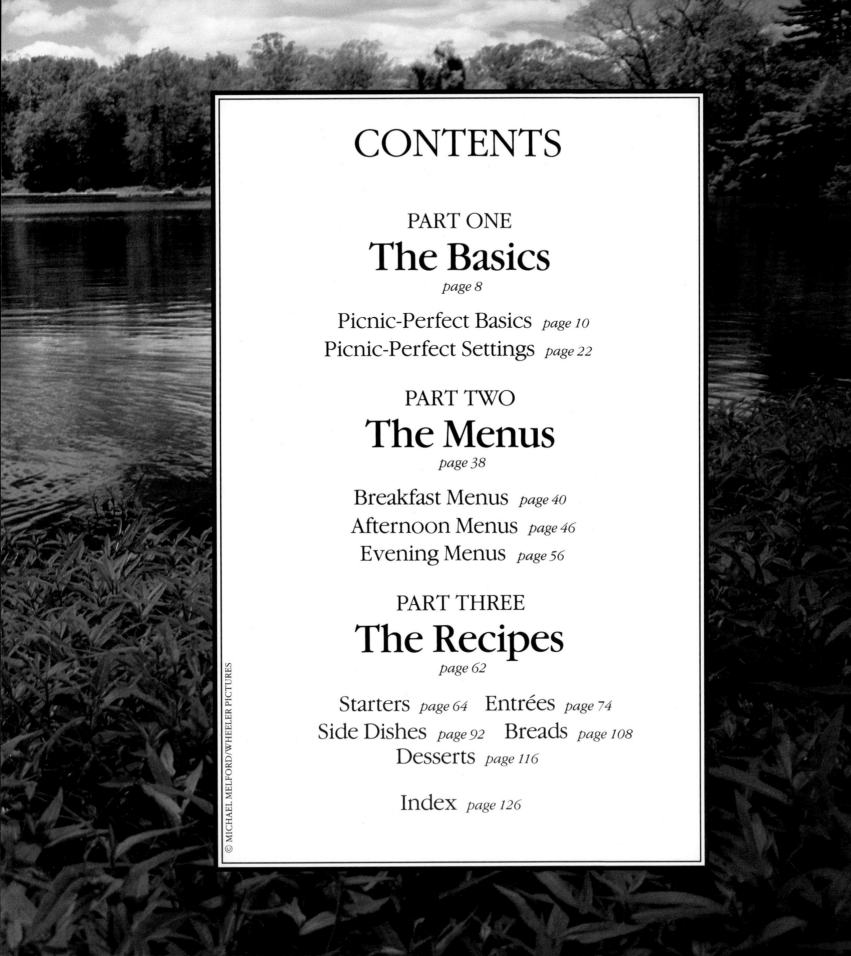

CONTENTS

PART ONE

The Basics
page 8

Picnic-Perfect Basics   *page 10*
Picnic-Perfect Settings   *page 22*

PART TWO

The Menus
page 38

Breakfast Menus   *page 40*
Afternoon Menus   *page 46*
Evening Menus   *page 56*

PART THREE

The Recipes
page 62

Starters   *page 64*   Entrées   *page 74*
Side Dishes   *page 92*   Breads   *page 108*
Desserts   *page 116*

Index   *page 126*

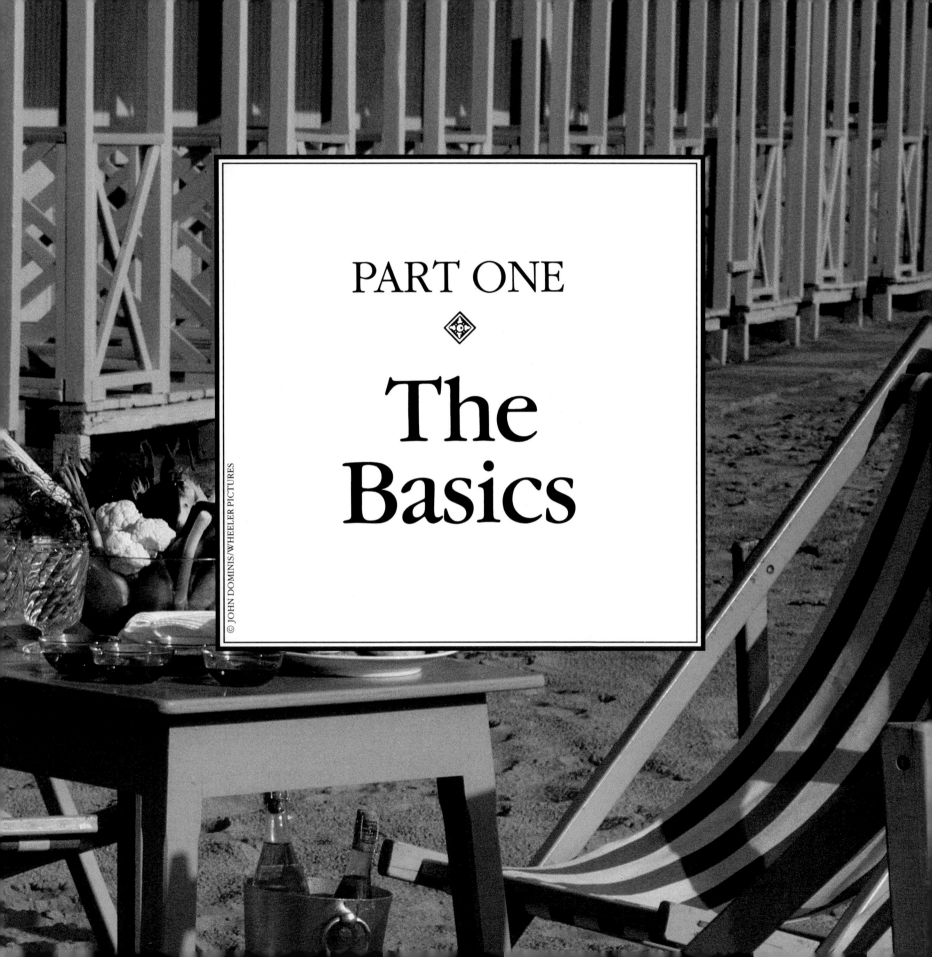

PART ONE

◆

The Basics

Picnic-Perfect Basics

Given enough equipment and staff, almost any food can be enjoyed outdoors. The British, for example, were known for putting together quite an elegant version of high tea, even on the road. Cucumber sandwiches, starched napery, and pots of boiling water went with them everywhere, including to great outdoor camps in India and Africa.

Today's alfresco event isn't nearly so elaborate, unless it's a catered affair and someone else is responsible for bringing the candelabra. Food, too, leans toward the manageable. Though the menu might venture beyond sandwiches and hot dogs, dining outdoors need not mean extensive planning and preparation. Picnics have relaxed considerably since the mid-1800s, when Mrs. Beeton, in her *Book of Household Management*, decreed that a proper picnic should consist of thirty-five different dishes. These days, picnic food should be easy to prepare. Even a fancy alfresco dinner loses its luster if the cook has been chained to the stove for days preparing it.

Foods That Keep Safely

© MICHAEL MELFORD/WHEELER PICTURES

In planning a picnic menu, it's a good idea to start with foods that can be made ahead of time and served either cold or at room temperature. Probably the best-known examples are fried chicken and potato salad.

Regrettably, someone must have gotten sick from this combination at one point and the blame was placed on the mayonnaise holding the potatoes together. The eggs in mayonnaise—when left at room temperature—were determined to be a perfect growing medium for dangerous microorganisms.

Fortunately, food scientists have leapt to the defense and set this erroneous rumor straight. After extensive testing, mayonnaise—or at least the commercial variety — has received a clean bill of health. In fact, according to the Food Research Institute at the University of Wisconsin, commercial mayonnaise both helps prevent the growth of salmonella and *Staphylococcus aureus* and reduces its presence in items like ham and chicken salad. All the vinegar, lemon or lime juice, salt, sugar, and citric or malic acid that goes into its preparation creates a hostile environment in which no harmful bacteria can grow.

So don't spare store-bought mayonnaise or any other salad dressing that contains significant amounts of vinegar, lemon juice, salt, or sugar. In fact, when preparing picnic dishes, it's a good idea to sauce them early, and chill them in the refrigerator so the bacterial fighting properties start working right away.

What may cause trouble is the way you handle the other ingredients that end up mixed with the mayonnaise. To avoid contaminating items like chicken, potatoes, and ham, remember the following tips:

• Don't give bacteria a place to lurk and a chance to spread. Scrub your hands before handling food and be-tween steps. Clean knives, cutting boards, and other utensils each time they come in contact with raw meats, eggs, fish, and poultry. Use clean sponges and dish cloths, or paper towels.

• Keep cold foods below 40° F. and chill thoroughly before packing in insulated containers to inhibit the growth of organisms. Thaw frozen foods and store marinating items in the refrigerator. Chill cooked foods as soon as they stop steaming. Add dressings early on and then finish cooling in the refrigerator.

• If the food is to be served hot, heat it to at least 140° F. before storing it in an insulated thermos. Don't pack cold and hot foods together.

• Outdoors, keep the food and cooler out of the direct sun. Before returning home, discard any perishables that have been at room temperature for several hours.

GORDON E. SMITH

© GEOFFREY CLIFFORD/WHEELER PICTURES

Foods That are Easy to Transport, Serve, and Eat

© JUDD PILOSSOF

Of course, the perfect picnic food is one that can be eaten out of hand. No wonder the sandwich travels to so many alfresco events. It's not only effortless to pack, it's also easy to eat.

Barbecued ribs, puréed soups, phyllo pastries, dips and crackers, deviled eggs, muffins, rolls, and cookies are all picnic foods in the hand-to-mouth category.

But many other items require only a fork or spoon to eat because the food is already in manageable pieces. These dishes include thick soups, the plethora of picnic salads (potato, shrimp, bean, chicken, rice, fruit, red pepper, macaroni, etc.), entrée and dessert pies, and cakes.

Last come those dishes that require a full complement of utensils. Many meats fall into this category, but even some of those can be managed with only a fork, if carved up before leaving home.

When choosing the food, consider the following:

Can it be put in a container easily? Soups and chili can slide directly into a thermos for transporting and can then be poured into serving dishes on the spot.

Salads and dips can be served with a spoon directly from bowls or jars. Deviled eggs can rest in an egg carton. Use jars or plastic containers with screw or snap lids for saucy dishes. Items that won't leak only need be covered with plastic wrap or aluminum foil, but remember that a certain amount of jostling goes with any traveling. Pies and tarts can be cut ahead of time and left in their baking tins for easy carrying.

Does it wrap conveniently? Take the piece whole when it comes to items such as pork tenderloin, gravlax, or flank steak, if you don't mind traveling with a sharp knife for carving. Though if you prefer, whole cuts of meats, and cakes may also be cut at home and reassembled into their original shapes before sealing in aluminum foil.

Stack flat foods for effortless packaging. Barbecued ribs, chicken pieces, cookies, and phyllo puffs all travel well resting on top of each other. Separate the layers with a piece of wax paper so the items don't stick together. Either wrap the stack in aluminum foil or, for extra security, pack in tins or boxes with tight lids.

GORDON E. SMITH

How to Keep Hot Foods Hot and Cold Foods Cold

COURTESY OF WILLIAMS-SONOMA

Keeping foods at their appropriate temperatures is easily done. Given the metal, plastic, and Styrofoam containers, coolers, and thermoses now on the market, almost any object can stay at a constant temperature for several hours. One such gizmo even allows the picnicker to tote along ice cubes.

Of course, the beauty of many of these new carrying devices is that they're both lightweight and durable. Once you figure out the sort of picnic fare you normally pack, an investment in this specialized equipment will make picnicking even more of a pleasure.

But no matter what piece of equipment you choose, three main rules of thumb apply to heating and cooling:

1. Begin by heating or cooling the food to its correct temperature.

2. Then store it in an insulated container that is already heated or chilled. This is particularly easy with thermos jars and chests that can be tempered with boiling or icy water 15 to 30 minutes before packing. Also remember that hot and cold foods must be packed in separate chests.

3. Finally, make sure the most perishable goods are closest to the ice and be careful not to crowd them. A little air circulation is beneficial, as is a shady spot for all the items to rest at the picnic site. If possible, pack those foods you'll eat first on top and work your way down during the meal. That saves unnecessary opening of the chest and helps everything stay at the right temperature for a longer period of time.

In general, cold foods travel best because ice is such an effective and easy cooling device. While a big hunk lasts longer than smaller pieces, all sizes work. Water frozen in a milk carton that has been taped shut makes a very effective medium-size block of ice.

Still, ice does eventually turn to water that sloshes about. Frozen gel packs, however, stay cold for long stretches of time, and the dissolved liquid remains in its container. On top of that, the gel packs can be refrozen for future use. Simply store them in your freezer between picnics. Also, as frozen boxes or cans of juice thaw, they conveniently keep other foods cool.

Food containers stay hot when tightly wrapped in eight or nine layers of newspaper. Hot ceramic tiles are another useful way to keep temperatures from cooling too rapidly. To keep something chilled, wrap it in wet newsprint for evaporative cooling. For even greater heat and cold retention, wrap the container in heavy-duty aluminum foil, then in paper, and finally place in an insulated bag or cover with a blanket.

As a last resort, remember that for a very small picnic, it's always possible to tie some ice in a plastic bag to bury the drinks. Leave room in the bag to put the cold food on top, cover with a quilt, and you're set to go.

See the individual Transportation Tips at the end of each recipe for instructions on handling that dish.

The Basics of Organizing the Picnic Basket

© MICHAEL MELFORD/WHEELER PICTURES

The first step in organizing any picnic basket is to draw up a list of what you'll need. This may be in your mind or on a piece of paper. It matters not, so long as all the tools and foods end up going with you.

For traumaless picnicking, serious alfresco diners keep crucial utensils and other assorted items permanently tucked in the basket.

In such a basket you're likely to find:

First aid supplies

Insect repellent

Candles and matches

Large and small knives and a cutting board

Bottle opener and corkscrew or Swiss army knife

Salt, pepper, and sugar cubes or packets

Paper towels, disposable washcloths, and garbage bags

You'll also need the basics of table setting. Many picnickers set aside a complete service for six solely for outdoor eating. This set may have come strapped inside an elegant English wicker hamper, or it could just as easily be a collection of 1940s Melmac dishes found at a yard sale.

Though you may not need every item every time, you'll eventually have use for:

Knives, forks, tablespoons, and teaspoons

Plates (possibly the ones with three compartments for different foods)

Bowls, including serving dishes

Mugs or cups and saucers

Glasses

Napkins

Tablecloth and ground cover

ELYSE LEWIN/KIM FREEMAN, STYLIST

SANDRA DOS PASSOS

Depending on whether your picnic is light or heavy, simple or swell, the table or ground setting should be changed to fit the mood. Sometimes plastic spoons and paper cups will be the answer, other times it might be appropriate to polish the silver and wrap the crystal.

When wrapping up items for the picnic basket, store the heavy, bulkier things on the bottom; fragile items go on top. Another good trick is to wrap things inside each other. For instance, individual settings of silverware can be wrapped in napkins, and bowls can nest inside one another.

Following the heavy to light rule of thumb, try to fill the basket so those items you'll need first are packed last. At a minimum, pack the tablecloth and ground cover last so they can act as a protective and decorative lid.

For those people who prefer to dine outdoors around a table, folding furniture should be added to the list of worthwhile equipment. One such item is a collapsible picnic table complete with four attached seats and a folding umbrella. It packs up into its own suitcase. Other options include beach chairs and bridge tables.

GORDON E. SMITH

Dealing with Insects and Other Intruders

When it comes to protecting the food, the best bet is to unpack and uncover it at the last moment. But sometimes you'd like to leave the food sitting out so people can nibble it at leisure. In that case, dishes that don't have lids of their own can be covered with tent-shaped netting devices. These handy, collapsible old-fashioned inventions come in several sizes to stand guard over both large and small containers. Also available are mesh bowls that can be turned upside down over plates of food.

If you want to be sure the pie doesn't get attacked by airborne insects, bake it in a ceramic dish that comes with its own appropriately decorated top. A covered pie dish has the additional advantage of being easy to pack and transport, and that, after all, is the object of the game.

It's unfortunate that more picnics don't take place in the late fall. The air may be a little chilly, but at least there aren't any ants or flies to bother you.

No one likes being at the mercy of a hovering dragon-fly and a colony of ants. So if your ecological sense won't be offended, spray the ground around your picnic spot with an insect repellent. Do, though, avoid spraying the table and food.

Additionally, it's a wise idea to dab or spray a similar substance on yourself. Flies, ticks, and chiggers are truly unnerving intruders capable of spoiling a perfectly beautiful day. In this case, being forearmed is a healthy precaution.

Picnic-Perfect Settings

For the Victorians, setting up a picnic wasn't much different from setting a table in the dining room. The silver, crystal, and china all got packed up and carted outdoors by the parlor maid and butler.

Then informality came into vogue, and paper goods entered the picnicker's life. Though they are sometimes a little flimsy, the great advantage of paper plates and cups is their light-weight impermanence. Cleaning up to go home is a breeze. Everything simply goes into the trash.

Plastic goods take those admirable qualities one step further. Being sturdy, unbreakable, and easy to carry, this modern material may be the single most important reason picnics have seen a renaissance in the last several years.

Given the incredible number of options, alfresco table settings have no trouble matching almost any outdoor mood. And since many paper and plastic utensils aren't particularly expensive, the whims of the picnic organizer can be easily satisfied without bankrupting the household budget.

New Twists on Paper and Plastic Products

© JEFF McNAMARA/JAMES GOSLEE III, STYLIST

At one time paper goods were notoriously boring and fragile. White ruled the day, and most often a paper plate was only substantial enough to hold a piece of cake.

Now paper comes in bright solid colors and attractive designs that rival elegant fine china. It also comes with a coated surface designed to repel moisture. No longer are paper plates a soggy mess by the time dinner is done. Just as important, paper products have acquired some heft—enough so that knife and fork dining can be accomplished without cutting straight through. To make paper plates even more sturdy, they can be placed in wicker holders specifically designed for this purpose.

Paper goods are best suited for a crowd; for sandwiches and items that won't run off the plate if it bends a bit; and for casual or themed affairs where you might enjoy the variety of designs now available.

Plastic is better suited for smaller gatherings since it does tend to cost a bit more; for meals where a knife and fork are required or when saucy items are prevalent; and for informal events that call for bright or dramatic colors.

Plastics have also entered a new phase. While this form of dinnerware was originally meant to last a lifetime, many of today's lightweight materials are designed and priced for temporary use only. This makes it possible for picnickers to affordably change plate patterns to suit any occasion.

As plastic plates have slimmed down, plastic tableware has become more substantial. At one time, picnickers considered themselves lucky if they negotiated a complete meal without breaking one of the plastic forks. Using a flimsy knife to cut anything tougher than a piece of pie was equally problematic. Now plastic cutlery has added stature and often gets tossed in the dishwasher for repeated use.

Some people are even turning to plastics for dinner at home. Nowhere is this more apparent than in glassware, especially in households with young children. Acrylic glasses have long come in tall and squat drinking-glass shapes, but lately it's also possible to buy clear, sturdy plastic champagne flutes and wine goblets.

Besides being shaped into plates, mugs, tumblers, and stemmed glasses, plastics are also the wave of the future in coolers, and other carrying devices.

GORDON E. SMITH

China and Silver Sparkle in the Sun or Under the Stars

© JOHN DOMINIS/WHEELER PICTURES

China is best saved for special, swell occasions—and especially romantic ones, when nothing but the gleam of the real thing will do. The gathering can be large or small, depending on the number of place settings you have and the strength of the people who will be helping to carry the baskets. Likewise, the setting and food can be formal or not. While it follows that china goes perfectly at a hunt country dinner picnic, there's nothing to say that it can't be packed for a breakfast on the beach.

Plates, being flat, are easy enough to pack since they can be stacked one on top of another or nestled side-by-side. The only trick is finding some sort of padding to rest between the layers to cushion any bumps and jolts .

Here paper or cloth napkins are perfect, as are tea towels. To wrap, place the plate in the center of the cloth and fold all four corners into the center. The edges are held down by the plate resting on top or next to it. The last plate gets wrapped upside down, so the flapping ends here are tucked underneath. Pack cups in the same manner. And remember that the china, being heavy, should be put in the bottom of hamper.

Silver, of course, requires no special treatment since it's unbreakable. It is, however, susceptible to getting lost and that's why many picnickers wrap each place setting in a separate napkin. That way, at least when leaving the house, everything is accounted for and secure. Another approach is to use a special silver carrying caddy.

The only way to be sure that all the utensils come back from the outing is to count them before leaving the site. It may seem compulsive, but if the silver belonged to your Aunt Mabs and is a pattern no longer being made, the effort is worth it.

Needless to say, all this packing will probably leave you with a fair number of extra napkins on your picnic. Should that be a bother, you might want to pack up the china and silver in the wrapping devices especially made for that purpose. Silver normally comes in a slotted cloth that not only wraps but also ties around the utensils. China storage is made extra easy with a vinyl, zippered case with felt pieces that are placed between the plates. Another alternative is to separate the plates with bubble wrap.

© FRED LYON/WHEELER PICTURES

Crystal Goes Outside: How to Pack It

COURTESY OF WILLIAMS-SONOMA

The perfect accompaniment to fine china is, of course, fine crystal. Especially for festive occasions—like engagement parties and symphony concerts—picnickers are once again willing to take the time to pack up the crystal. After all, drinking champagne from an acrylic flute is one thing. Sipping it out of a finely cut glass is something else entirely. The only catch is making sure the Waterford doesn't get broken en route.

Packing up glasses isn't nearly as traumatic as one might expect. Simply wrap each glass individually. For a picnic, wrapping crystal in paper towels or large paper napkins is a good bet, and in a pinch the paper goods can be used to mop up a spill. Another trick is to wrap fine glasses in cloth napkins.

In either case, lay the glass on its side in the middle of the cloth, with the ends of the glass pointing from corner to corner. Stuff one of the corners inside the glass, fold the opposite corner up over the glass, and roll the napkin up around the glass from one of the remaining corners to the other.

If the glasses have stems, pack them side by side, the bowl of one resting against the stem of another. Additionally, wrap these in a tablecloth so the glasses have extra padding on top and bottom. For best results, place glasses at the top of the picnic hamper or, better yet, in a separate box.

When it comes to matching up silverware and glasses, the best guideline is to keep it all in the same general family. Heavy-duty plastic utensils and cups go with paper and plastic plates. Combination stainless-plastic utensils and acrylic glasses go with the more substantial and permanent plastics. The silver service (or possibly stainless) is most appropriate for china and crystal.

Ground Covers and Other Linens

GORDON E. SMITH

Old-fashioned handmade quilts probably make the best multifunctional ground covers. First, they're made from cloth so they have the feel and washability of table linen. Next, they are colorful and attractive. Finally, they have a little padding to make sitting easier.

On dry, grassy ground, however, all you'll need is a large tablecloth, though it's advisable to place another cloth or blanket on the ground beneath any linen you think might be damaged by grass stains. Should you have only placemats, simply use the blanket all by itself.

Embroidered or lacy tablecloths are a perfect match for china and silver. Marimekko printed sheets and cloths work well with primary-color plastic plates. A cotton-backed vinyl cloth or woven tatami mat is just the ticket for when paper plates are being used.

All of these ground covers and linens also work well draped over a picnic table, as do paper cloths. While there's a certain romance to spreading your picnic out on the ground, tabletop eating does have its advantages.

To begin with, you can bring along push pins (or tape) to secure the covering if it's a windy day. With a sturdy surface you also don't have the problem of tipping glasses and spilled bottles of wine.

Should you opt for the lawn instead, consider investing in a space blanket for the primary cover. These lightweight ground covers are available at sporting goods and outdoor equipment stores. One side is shiny and reflects heat. The other is dull and absorbs it. So if the ground is a little chilly or damp, put the shiny side up. Your body heat will be reflected, and you'll stay warm. Put the dull side up when both you and the ground are hot and you want to stay cool.

© FRED LYON/WHEELER PICTURES

What to Pack It Up In

COURTESY OF CRATE & BARREL

In general, picnic carrying devices now come in two forms. For tradition-conscious picnickers, there are wicker and woven baskets. For the more modern individual, nylon, canvas or hemp bags are exceedingly popular. Both types do their jobs admirably.

Those who use wicker or woven wood like its lightweight yet sturdy, defined shape and substantive feel. Baskets are best for packing items that need some protection (like the china) or stability from shifting back and forth (like most foods).

Some of these baskets are open at the top, others have lids, and many have a separate place to stash a long loaf of bread or a bottle of wine. A few come equipped with a thermos or two for carrying hot and cold items.

Because they have shape and strength, wicker baskets can be quite substantial, though smaller, over-the-arm versions are popular also. The size you choose depends on your budget and the kind of picnicking you do.

Picnic bags are normally lightweight with collapsible sides, though newer nylon types now use foam side panels for added shape. Even with extra substance, nylon bags still feel less stable than wicker baskets, and this also holds true for canvas and hemp totes.

All of these bags are, however, just as strong as wicker baskets. With this sturdiness they serve well carrying bulky, heavy items (like blankets and thermos bottles) and items that aren't in danger of tipping or breaking (like the candlestick holder and plastic and paper goods).

COURTESY OF CRATE & BARREL

Complete Picnic Sets

COURTESY OF WILLIAMS-SONOMA

COURTESY OF CRATE & BARREL

Picnic sets are for the person who picnics often and feels strongly that there should be a place for everything with everything in its place. These contained units include not only the carrying basket, but also glasses, plates, cups, and silver. Depending on the size of the basket and its particular emphasis, you may also find tucked away napkins and tablecloth, wine glasses and corkscrew, knife and cutting board or a thermos or two.

Though picnic sets used to be available only with wicker carrying cases, many of the new collections are housed in nylon carryalls. With foam sides, these have some shape, yet are amazingly easy to carry and pack.

COURTESY OF WILLIAMS-SONOMA

On-Site Grilling

Though some picnickers prefer to prepare all food in advance, many find a special pleasure in cooking on the spot in the open air.

Most people are used to barbecuing or grilling only in the back yard or at designated picnic or camp sites. That's not to say, however, that you can't take your grill with you. The old stand-by, the hibachi, is small, sturdy, and easily carried. Even given all the new grilling equipment to come on the market lately, it continues to be one of the most durable and portable open-fire cooking devices.

Available in several sizes—for small- and medium-sized households— it is a model of efficient fire building and heat distribution. Made in Japan where fuel was, for a long time, at a premium, this squat heat source rests close to the ground or can be placed on top of a sturdy table. The grill itself has a handle so it can be moved closer to or further from the coals.

Another Japanese cooking unit, called the Tokyo grill, cooks meat and vegetables on a flatiron griddle. It has a round surface and is designed for communal table-top cooking.

If you don't need something this sturdy for your picnic cooking or if you won't have time for the heavy grill to cool down, consider the thin metal fold-up version. When its legs are extended, it looks similar to a bed tray. This lightweight grill rests over an open fire and is the answer to painless portability when the picnic site isn't right next to the car.

There's nothing worse than having a fire that won't start or one that dies too soon. So, don't forget to take along a sufficient supply of briquets, lighter fluid, and matches. In addition, gloves or pot holders, as well as long-handled tongs and spatulas, should be added to your list in order to make cooking easier and safer.

© JOHN DOMINIS/WHEELER PICTURES

© JUDD PILOSSOF

Coolers and Thermoses

COURTESY OF WILLIAMS-SONOMA

If plastic tableware has given a shot in the arm to dining alfresco, so have plastic coolers and thermoses. Now not only do food and drinks remain hot and cold, but carrying them about the countryside causes minimal strain.

This isn't to say that metal heating and cooling devices aren't effective and long lasting. That they are. But toting them about is a cumbersome task.

With the age of plastic and nylon, the cooler and thermos have been freed to take on amazing new shapes and configurations. Specialization is now the byword.

Naturally the bigger, traditional-size cooler popular with campers continues to be available. But you also can find nylon cases with plastic insulated linings suitable for carrying trays of ice. For those who are tired of rummaging around in cold water to find the beer, another pack carries six cans in a tube that is easily slung over the shoulder. Or should you only have wine to chill, that's possible too in a tall, two-pocket carrying case with a freezable wall divider.

When it comes to thermoses, there are almost no bounds. Some pour, some pump, and others operate with an old-fashioned spigot. For thicker liquids, there are short and tall as well as narrow- and wide-mouthed jars. Many have straps for carrying over the shoulder; others stand alone. Some even appear in tandem, with two thermoses in one carrying container.

One of the most novel, however, is the thermos that lets you pack up a three-course meal. Removable individual sections make it possible to seal three different foods in their own leakproof compartments. One of the sections is even insulated to retain heat or cold. The unit comes complete with a spoon and a carrying strap. The only thing it lacks is the food.

JEFF McNAMARA

Lighting and Decoration Ideas

GORDON E. SMITH

While lighting your picnic isn't an issue in the daytime, the topic may arise if you like dining outdoors in the evening. Should this late-hour picnic take place on the patio, chances are electricity will be fairly close by. But going further afield most likely will require candles.

Fortunately, outdoor candles now come in so many different shapes and sizes that it may be difficult to choose.

There are long tapers that stick in the ground that both give light and drive away the insects. Other candles, surrounded by glass globes, come perched at the end of metal rods which poke into the ground.

Candles also come in clay and glazed pots so light breezes won't blow them out, and for the old-fashioned picnic there's the oil lantern with the tall chimney.

Romantics, however, probably will opt for a small candelabrum or even a simple candle holder with one long taper. These are traditionally the classic approach to intimate lighting, and the effect is worth it, especially if your picnic is taking place at dusk when light really isn't the issue.

If your picnic happens to be in the backyard, but you'd rather not turn on the lights, consider a votive candle in a paper bag. To create this lovely light source, fill a medium-size paper bag with a small amount of sand or pea gravel to hold it in place. Then place a lighted votive candle in the bag and on the sand or gravel. The light it throws off is soft and delicate, and because the candle is protected by its paper bag chimney the light won't blow out. And, never fear, the bag will not catch fire.

But lights are only one form of decoration. A small bouquet of flowers always adds a nice touch. Or if you know there'll be wild flowers where you plan to picnic, simply carry along a vase to put them in.

For a more celebratory touch, balloons grounded in a pot of dirt or tied to a rock are a festive way to identify your table in a crowded area. Hand-lettered banners are another attractive way to make your picnic special or announce someone's birthday.

For the national holiday, consider propping a flag in the ground or festooning bunting from the branches of a nearby tree. And when you head down to the shore, don't forget to take along a colorful, fold-up beach umbrella.

COURTESY OF WILLIAMS-SONOMA

Packing Up and Going Home

COURTESY OF WILLIAMS-SONOMA

This is where paper towels, disposable washcloths, and plastic garbage bags come in handy. Without them the aftermath of alfresco dining wouldn't be nearly so painless. As mentioned earlier, they're indispensable basics for picnickers.

For one thing, paper and other disposable plastic and tin items simply get tied up in a bag and left on the spot in a trash bin, never to be seen again. What could be easier? In fact, you should do the same thing with most of the leftover food since prolonged periods in the sun make it unsafe for eating later.

That means you'll be left with only the serving dishes and any utensils, china or glassware brought along. Most of these items can be wiped with paper towels or disposable wash cloths before repacking. Remember, you're not trying to wash anything now. All you're doing is removing big blobs of food.

Should no trash bin be handy, you'll need to take the garbage bag home with you, but since it's sealed and leakproof, that shouldn't be a problem.

The only item of special concern when returning home is packing the china and crystal so no breakage occurs. Many people simply wrap it up in the napkins and tablecloths it came in. Another method would be to carry along the day's newspaper and wrap the dirty dishes in that in order to save a little wear and tear on the linen. Having the morning edition handy also gives you something to do in that glorious time after any outdoor meal when people doze and read and remember just how perfect a picnic can be.

PART TWO

❖

The Menus

© JOHN DOMINIS/WHEELER PICTURES

Breakfast Menus

The breakfast picnic. For those who, literally, wake at the crack of dawn. For those who are up and out early anyway, running through the park or cycling along the river. And for those who can't find any other portion of the day that isn't already booked.

With breakfasts making a comeback, this is only the next logical step. Besides that, mornings are beautiful and refreshing. It's a perfect time to be outdoors—and in the height of summer, that's saying something.

Most of these menus should be started in advance. All of the foods keep well—even the muffins—and some items actually need a day or two in the refrigerator, to cure or marinate. No need here to get up in the middle of the night to bake the bread or mix up the cucumbers.

An asterisk (*) next to an item in a menu indicates that a recipe is included in Part Three.

Elegant and Easy

Whether you call it lox, gravlax, or smoked salmon, it's a weekend breakfast tradition when paired with bagels. Buy it at a specialty food store, or, given a couple of days notice, you can easily cure the salmon yourself. The chopped tomatoes that are so often served alongside appear here as a separate dish with cucumbers.

When you pack up, be sure to remember a sharp knife and a small cutting board for the salmon. Of course, you could carve it ahead of time, but half the fun of gravlax is that everyone gets an opportunity to slice it, nibbling away at the the paper-thin shavings in the process.

Obviously, you'll want to split and toast the bagels before packing up, and there are even special ceramic tiles that can be heated to help keep your bagels warm. Don't, however, combine the strawberries and sugar. Instead just lightly rinse the berries and carry them in a berry bowl. Take the confectioner's sugar in either a metal dusting canister or an elegant crystal muffineer.

Gravlax with Sour Cream Mustard Sauce*

Bagels

Dilled Tomatoes and Cucumbers*

Strawberries Dipped in Confectioners' Sugar

Champagne

Coffee

Cosmopolitan Beginnings

Not exactly a breakfast smorgasbord, but you can pretend. Start with the cucumber version of the Bloody Mary, then dip into the deviled eggs and finish with bite-sized sandwiches of ham and Jarlsberg. It's a delightful progression of flavors.

Make the sandwiches ahead of time or have the butcher do the slicing and your guests do the serving, leaving you only the task of baking the rolls. Spoons are the only item you'll need here, unless you press your guests into action. Then bring along a couple of knives and forks for serving.

Of course, you'll want to keep the soup chilled in an insulated container. Should you want to serve the sandwiches warm, wrap them individually in aluminum foil, heat the food packages in the oven briefly, and immediately store them in a thermos chest.

Cucumber Soup* Laced with Vodka

Deviled Eggs*

Pocketbook Rolls* and Butter

Thinly Sliced Baked Danish Ham and Jarlsberg

Copenhagen Blend Coffee

Sophisticated Love Affair

Papayas and peaches combine with a honey dressing in a monochromatic marvel of delicacy. For punch and definition in this menu, look to the prosciutto and Gorgonzola—and the Italian roast coffee.

Fortunately this menu is as sophisticated as it is easy to prepare. The only culinary challenge here comes with the soda crackers, and if you find that more than you want to tackle, simply purchase a good, imported biscuit at the market.

Don't forget to bring spoons for the fruit and knives for the Gorgonzola, but you won't need anything sharp, since the prosciutto will come sliced.

Sliced Papaya and Peaches with Honey Dressing*

Prosciutto

Gorgonzola

Plain Soda Crackers*

Italian Roast Coffee

Baked Goods Bonanza

When a Continental breakfast is all you require, this is the one to take down to the park with the morning paper. Start with a hearty tomato-cucumber mix laced with vodka, end with coffee, and nibble a sampling of sweets along the way.

The muffins will feel healthy, the buttered cinnamon-nut loaf triangles will feel European, and the peanut butter and banana cake sandwiches with cream cheese will remind you of a cozy childhood.

All here is finger food, though you may want to bring knives and butter for the muffins. Other than that, just remember glasses for the Bloody Marys and mugs for the coffee.

Bloody Marys* Laced with Vodka

Oatmeal Spice Muffins*

Buttered Cinnamon-Nut Loaf Triangles*

Peanut Butter and Banana Cake* Sandwiches with
Cream Cheese

Vienna Roast Coffee

Hearty Fare

After a morning hike, this is just what you need—besides maybe a cool shower. The cheese and potato pie will stick to your ribs. The melon balls will refresh your spirit.

The pie travels nicely in its own pan, and the melon balls can slosh comfortably in the sauce. Just don't forget serving utensils and a knife to cut the pie (though you could do that at home).

Jarlsberg and Potato Pie*

Melon Balls with Raspberry Sauce*

White Wine

Breakfast on the Beach

This menu should be served when the hike you plan to take is across the sand dunes to the beach.

Goodness knows the tomato soup will be refreshing after you've worked up a dewy brow. But don't expect great weight—just depth of character—from the onion and ricotta pie. It is there mainly to delight your taste buds.

Cut the pie ahead, if you like, but carry it in the pan with the sides in place. It's just easier that way. Spoons and forks are required here, as well as serving cutlery.

Cold Tomato Soup with Cucumber*

Onion and Ricotta Pie*

Coffee

Feeding the Multitudes

After the race, why not let your running partners straggle back to your car for a nibble and a chat to find out who did what. Since the phyllo dough makes plenty of puffs, you'll only need to double the recipes for the cucumbers and tomatoes and the deviled eggs. Fortunately, all this can be done the night before.

Even though this is mainly finger food, remember small plates and forks for the cucumbers and tomatoes.

Ham and Cheese Puffs in Phyllo*

Dilled Tomatoes and Cucumbers*

Deviled Eggs*

White Wine

Afternoon Menus

The afternoon picnic. When nothing beats being outdoors, reveling in spring flowers or fall football. When the family gathers to celebrate and the children can let loose with abandon. Or quite simply when all's right with the world—love's at hand and the wind's in your sail.

This is the time for a memorable menu, even if it isn't a particularly complicated one. Since you may not have time to make everything the morning of the event, prepare a couple of the recipes a day or two in advance. All keep well, and some actually improve with age.

Also be sure to have utensils and dishes in order so that packing up is a smooth operation. Many of the new plastic insulated containers will come in handy here to keep foods at their suggested temperature, though most of these recipes do just fine when served at room temperature.

An asterisk (*) next to an item in a menu indicates that a recipe is included in Part Three.

Before the Mast

Even if you don't get roped into sheeting in the jib, day sailing can work up an appetite. Actually, any contact with the water seems invigorating and calls for a little something to nibble as the day progresses.

Approach the ricotta pie and tomatoes and cucumbers at the first sign of boredom or mutiny. And break out the chocolate malted cake when you can no longer stand the thought of having an uneaten dessert around.

Much of this is finger food, including the pie if it's cut into small pieces, though it would help to have forks handy for the tomatoes and cucumbers.

Onion and Ricotta Pie*

Dilled Tomatoes and Cucumbers*

Chocolate Malted Cake*

Blush Wine

Take a Hike

When you can afford the weight of taking along something more than chipped beef, consider a hearty chili for a nippy afternoon. Chili, cornmeal muffins, and molasses sugar cookies make a soul-satisfying, stick-to-the-ribs combination.

The only disadvantage of this menu is that it requires a thermos big enough to store the chili. Otherwise, the muffins and cookies are a breeze to carry along. The beer, of course, is optional, though long insulated tubes that sling over the shoulder are making it more convenient to carry canned beverages.

Just don't forget cups and spoons for the chili and butter and knives for the muffins.

Chili Molé*

Cornmeal Muffins*

Chewy Molasses Sugar Cookies*

Beer

Afternoon in the Park

This cheese and potato pie has a nutty, creamy flavor that will be welcome in late spring or early fall when a meal of some substance is in order. It's the sort of fare you'd welcome after a walk in the woods.

The pie can be cut before setting out, but keep it in the plate, since that makes a perfect carrying and serving dish—especially if you've baked it in a ceramic dish that comes with a cover. It's a fork meal—mainly because of the green beans and cantaloupe. The pie, if cut into thin slices, is sturdy enough to eat with the fingers.

Jarlsberg and Potato Pie*

Green Beans with Basil Dressing*

Cantaloupe Wedges

Sugar Cookies*

Iced Coffee with Cream

Food Afloat

Life's easiest water adventure is an inner-tube float down a lazy river. But even those who go tubing carry something for noshing along the way.

Sandwiches are always popular as a menu staple, but if you can pull off to a sand bar and park your tube for a while, munching on cream cheese and olive macaroni salad is marvelously satisfying. The tomatoes with fresh basil are merely window dressing. The peanut butter and banana cake can be considered a midafternoon snack.

This menu does require a fork and plate or shallow bowl, but plastic ones are light, and in addition, they float.

Pimiento Cheese Sandwiches on Herb-Cheese Pullman Loaf*

Cream Cheese and Olive Macaroni Salad*

Sliced Tomatoes with Fresh Basil*

Peanut Butter and Banana Cake*

White Wine

You *Can* Take It with You

The experienced hiker—especially one who can no longer abide the thought of freeze-dried food—is most likely to be tempted by the solid feel of carrot soup, pasta salad, and fruit for dessert. It's just the sort of meal you'd serve indoors, yet it's one that carries with little strain as long as all the containers seal tightly.

At a minimum you'll need spoons and shallow bowls, though forks and plates would be useful also.

Carrot and Leek Soup*

Caesar Pasta Salad with Tuna*

Fruit Salad with Honey Dressing*

Iced Tea

On a Tailgate

Rumor has it that the station wagon was invented by a football fan who wanted his stadium parking lot picnic at table height. And surely that's a decided advantage of the tailgate. But this particular vehicle also has enough room to store comfortably a small grill for cooking the ribs that are the highlight of this pregame fan fare.

Unfortunately, cooking over coals before a football game is a mixed blessing. It does give you a project while standing around, chinning with your neighbors, but it is also a clear indication that you've got something good to eat. To keep things more circumspect, cook the ribs in the oven at home, wrap them tightly in heavy foil, and store in an insulated chest to hold the temperature.

This is a fork-and-finger dinner.

Baby Back Ribs with Barbecue Sauce*

Cole Slaw*

Red Pepper Salad*

Chewy Molasses Sugar Cookies*

Beer

Football Frenzy

A ham and cheese sandwich by itself might seem meager fare for the heartiness of a football game, but when it's combined with a butternut apple soup and sweet potato salad, you're talking substantial—and delicious, too.

Fortunately, the soup is puréed so it can be sipped from a mug while everyone is standing about. Then serve the sandwiches and sweet potato salad on a plate, finishing with bite-sized toffee bars and coffee.

Carry the soup in a thermos so it stays hot, and leave everything else at outdoor temperature—except, of course, the beverages.

Butternut Apple Soup*

Sliced Ham and Cheese Sandwiches on Herb-Cheese Pullman Loaf*

Sweet Potato Salad with Pineapple and Raisins*

Toffee Bars*

Beer

Coffee

Trysting Twosome

Romantics deserve a complex and subtle menu. Starting with a refreshing and zesty gazpacho, the rest of this meal meanders from a smooth, chilled salmon terrine laced with scallops to a wedge-cut and jacketed new potato salad to a creamy peach tart with a crisp, sugary crust.

Because this repast requires a full complement of cutlery, you might consider using the china and crystal instead of paper or plastic. Other than that, traveling is easy. The only item needing special attention is the soup, which you'll want to keep chilled.

Make half the recipe for the soup and potato salad, if you like, though you might be sorry. Remaining portions are usually quickly dispatched.

Cold Tomato Soup with Cucumber*

Salmon Terrine with Bay Scallops*

New Potato Salad*

Peach and Cream Cheese Tart*

White Wine

Easy and Impressive

If you don't make the whole-wheat rolls yourself, this menu can be organized in a flash. After quick stops at the fish and cheese markets and the grocery store, preparation—in large measure—hinges on can opening and food processing, with a brief foray into poaching, mixing, and baking.

The presentation of this knife-and-fork meal is, however, significantly more impressive than the time spent in the kitchen would indicate. Try to keep the tuna and cucumber sauce cool before serving, but should everything warm up along the way, that is fine also.

Whole-Wheat Rolls with Sunflower Kernels*

Goat Cheese

Poached Tuna with Cucumber Sauce*

Savory Bean Salad*

Chocolate Raspberry Bars with Walnuts*

Red Wine

International and Eclectic

This mixed bag of a menu combines Mexican, Indian, and English flavors. The first half of the meal is designed to pep you up, with seasonings adjusted to individual preference. The last half should serve to cool you down. What pulls it all together is the white wine.

Knives and forks are required for this late spring menu that draws on fresh, pencil-thin asparagus and juicy, ripe strawberries. And because it's a special kind of meal, add to the occasion with an unusual tablecloth, possibly something with a Mexican or Indian flare.

Guacamole with Pistachios*

Cornmeal Soda Crackers*

Curried Chicken Salad with Grapes* on Bibb Lettuce

Asparagus in Lemon Sauce*

Rolled Lime Curd Cake with Strawberry Sauce*

White Wine

Old-Fashioned Love

When the love of your life likes old-fashioned favorites, yet has enough curiosity to try something new, serve up this colorful autumnal menu. The green soup is a reminder of the summer past; the red and yellow peppers in the rice salad are reminiscent of the changing colors on the leaves. The golden roasted chicken and the crisp slivers of red in the apple tart speak for themselves.

Bring along a sharp knife to cut up the chicken and the tart on the spot or do this handy work before packing up. Also remember to bring the table knives, forks and spoons—this is an elegant meal.

If you like, prepare half portions of the soup and salad.

Watercress and Leek Soup*

Roasted Chicken* or Chicken Roasted on a Grill*

Rice Salad with Red and Yellow Peppers*

Apple Tart*

White Wine

Kids on the Loose

If your kids consider anything beyond bologna mystery meat, you may have trouble tempting them with flank steak sandwiches. But if they have a somewhat broader palate and won't think it funny that the meat and leafy greens are combined, this should be a welcome change.

However, if you want to keep this menu totally tame, make the sandwich loaf without the rolled filling and cook the flank steak flat and unstuffed. Of course, thin slices of it are in order either way it's prepared—a task that can be done at home or when you get to the picnic site.

Cut the tart before packing up, but slip the ring back around the springform pan for easy carrying.

Flank Steak Sandwiches on Herb-Cheese Pullman Loaf*

Savory Bean Salad*

Peach and Cream Cheese Tart*

Lemon/Lime Soda Pop

White Wine

Rosy Fare

Rosy to red is the tone of this meal. Even the mushrooms will take on a blush after they've rested in the marinade. Pack up this menu for a summer city picnic when radishes, tomatoes, and red peppers are at their finest.

Forks are required here, though the shrimp salad can be pocketed in the rolls, to be served as finger food. If, instead, you'd like to turn this into something more formal, mound the shrimp in a tomato that's been cut into wedges that stop short of going through the base.

Only worry about keeping the shrimp and wine cool—everything else tastes fine if it warms up.

Study in Red Shrimp Salad*

Pocketbook Rolls*

Sliced Tomatoes*

Rosy Marinated Mushrooms*

Toffee Bars*

Blush Wine

Evening Menus

The evening picnic. Because special activities draw us outside to sit on the lawn—listening to music or the sounds of a neighborhood bustling with good cheer. Because the longer days invite walking in the surf or at least lazing on the deck beyond the glass doors. And because it's finally cooled down.

Since you've had a good portion of the day to plan this event, the menu can be somewhat more elaborate. To avoid a frenetic, last-minute whirl in the kitchen, however, it's advisable to prepare two or three of the recipes a day or so in advance. All of these items keep well, and some actually benefit from the blending of flavors that comes from sitting around.

Given that the evening picnic is often tied to a special occasion and because it's usually a meal that requires a full set of eating utensils, plan on packing up the china and silver or its modern-day equivalent made from heavy-duty, colorful plastic. There's nothing more unnerving than a beautiful meal that wobbles around on a flimsy plate. Equally frustrating are knives and forks inadequate for the task. And worst of all is trying to eat dinner when the utensils were left at home.

Glassware is, of course, always appropriate, but with acrylic wine and champagne glasses being so commonplace, that route might be the safer and saner approach to take.

An asterisk (*) next to an item in a menu indicates that a recipe is included in Part Three.

Up-Scale Down-Home

It's hard to top fried chicken and apple pie as old-fashioned favorites. In this menu, however, they've been updated to give them new definition. The chicken here is boned and lightly breaded with ground almonds. The apple tart is an open-faced affair with the pastry and sliced apples appearing in a pizza pan. To go with the chicken, there's a luscious sweet potato salad and rosy-hued marinated mushrooms.

It's a menu that doesn't require chilling, except for the wine and, if you prefer, the chicken.

Almond Fried Chicken*

Sweet Potato Salad with Pineapple and Raisins*

Rosy Marinated Mushrooms*

Apple Tart*

White Wine

Tender Moments

If falling in love makes you feel like an adolescent, this menu should be appropriate, since the first part, at least, may remind you of your youth. Ah yes, salmon loaf and cream cheese and olive sandwiches. Only here they've taken on new life in the form of a cold terrine and a macaroni salad. The basic tastes, however, remain the same. Then to jar you into adulthood, there's a sophisticated red pepper salad and a sublime lime curd cake with raspberry sauce.

This meal travels well for several hours without refrigeration. And the macaroni salad, in particular, needs to warm up before serving. Make half the recipe for the salads, if you like.

If there are just the two of you, take only half the cake and be sure to bring along a sharp knife.

Salmon Terrine with Bay Scallops*

Cream Cheese and Olive Macaroni Salad*

Red Pepper Salad*

Rolled Lime Curd Cake with Raspberry Sauce*

White Wine

Color Contrasts

The flank steak in this menu, cut in thick slices, is a beautiful contrast of dark green spinach and slightly pink beef. The ratatouille also blends deeper shades, here enlivened with specks of red. Then to brighten the plate, serve delicately golden cornmeal muffins. With the addition of butter, these add considerable good cheer and taste.

Flank Steak Florentine*

Ratatouille*

Cornmeal Muffins*

Chocolate Malted Cake*

Red Wine

Fired Up

A barbecue is a leisurely, relaxed approach to the evening meal. This menu is for the bigger event that calls for something substantial like a leg of lamb. Here it is butterflied and rests in a pineapple-lemon juice and honey marinade that adds a sweet/tart taste to the lamb that is most becoming. If you're more inclined to finger food, slice and skewer the boned lamb before dropping it into the marinade.

Serve this in late summer or early fall when eggplant is in season and green beans are once again small. Because the dishes here all have some force, the chocolate malted cake is a logical choice for dessert.

Don't forget a sharp knife and carving board for slicing the lamb once it's cooked.

Grilled Leg of Lamb* or Grilled Lamb on a Stick*

Ratatouille*

Green Beans with Basil Dressing*

Whole-Wheat Rolls with Sunflower Kernels*

Chocolate Malted Cake*

Red Wine

Decked Out

Eating on the deck is the best of both worlds, since you're simultaneously at home and out of doors. But instead of treating this occasion like a normal dinner that happens to get moved outside, plan it like a picnic with foods that are intentionally done up ahead of time and served warm.

This menu happens to be perfect for fall, when apple cider and sweet potatoes are plentiful. The mushrooms and chocolate cake, of course, have no season.

And even though everything is handy with the kitchen nearby, you still might want to use a grill instead for cooking the meat.

Apple Glazed Pork Tenderloin* or Barbecued Whole
Pork Tenderloin*

Sweet Potato Salad with Pineapple and Raisins*

Rosy Marinated Mushrooms*

Chocolate Malted Cake*

Blush Wine

Chocolate is for Lovers

No doubt a menu of all chocolate would be appropriate for any couple in love, but sanity has to take over at some point. Here chocolate makes a modest showing only at dessert. Don't be fooled, however. This isn't weak-kneed chocolate, and especially not when it's combined with raspberry jam and walnuts.

Leading up to this dramatic conclusion is an equally sensational main course of unique, forceful flavors. The sweet touch of basil and fennel in the green beans blends nicely with the sweet bell peppers in the rice salad, and both of those are held in check by the salmon with cucumber sauce.

The salmon should probably be stored in a cold spot—along with the wine—but the rest of the menu can be served warm.

Poached Salmon with Cucumber Sauce*

Green Beans with Basil Dressing*

Rice Salad with Red and Yellow Peppers*

Chocolate Raspberry Bars with Walnuts*

White Wine

Block Party

When there are many mouths to feed, spinach puffs in phyllo go a long way toward making lots of people happy. And by doubling the chicken and rice salads and the marinated carrots, you'll be able to feed at least a portion of the block with little problem unless you live in an apartment building.

Worry only about keeping the chicken and wine cool. Everything else can stay at outside temperatures.

Double the chicken and rice salads and sauced carrots in order to feed twelve comfortably.

Spinach Puffs in Phyllo*

Curried Chicken Salad with Grapes*

Rice Salad with Red and Yellow Peppers*

Sauced Carrots, Zucchini, and Red Onions*

Sugar Cookies*

White Wine

Music in the Air

When the symphony starts the summer season—or when the municipal band sets up in the shell at the park—you'll want to celebrate the occasion with an elegant dinner on the lawn.

Fitting that bill nicely is this pasta salad with scallops, carrots, and celery. Just be sure to let it warm up before serving so the sauce has a chance to soften and the flavors come back to life.

Since it's an early summer menu, the soup can be served hot or cold, depending on your mood and the temperature outside.

Cut up the tart before heading off. You may also want to take only a portion of it on the trip.

If you'd rather not have leftovers, make smaller portions of the soup, pasta and asparagus.

Watercress and Leek Soup*

Creamy Corkscrew Pasta with Scallops and Vegetables*

Asparagus in Lemon Sauce*

Peach and Cream Cheese Tart*

White Wine

PART THREE

◆

The Recipes

© JOHN DOMINIS/WHEELER PICTURES

STARTERS

COLD TOMATO SOUP WITH CUCUMBER
COLD TOMATO SAUCE
BLOODY MARY
BUTTERNUT APPLE SOUP
CARROT AND LEEK SOUP
WATERCRESS AND LEEK SOUP
GUACAMOLE WITH PISTACHIOS
ROSY MARINATED MUSHROOMS
GRAVLAX WITH
SOUR CREAM MUSTARD SAUCE
PIMIENTO CHEESE
SPINACH PUFFS IN PHYLLO
HAM AND CHEESE PUFFS
IN PHYLLO

Cold Tomato Soup with Cucumber

Make this at the height of summer when luscious and juicy tomatoes are perfect and plentiful. It's a refreshing, hearty, and uncomplicated gazpacho that's thick enough to eat with a spoon. Because of its chunkiness, it also does delightful double duty as a tomato sauce. Or try it thinned with additional tomato juice to add new dimension to a Bloody Mary.

6 ripe medium tomatoes
1 medium cucumber
6 medium scallions
1 slice white bread
1/2 cup tomato purée
2 cups tomato juice
1 teaspoon red wine vinegar
1 tablespoon olive oil
1 small garlic clove, peeled and trimmed
1/2 to 1 teaspoon salt
1/2 teaspoon granulated sugar

1. Place the tomatoes in a large saucepan of boiling water, remove from the heat, and let rest 2 or 3 minutes until the skins begin to crack. Lift the tomatoes out of the water with a slotted spoon, cool briefly, and peel. Cut in half crosswise and squeeze out the seeds.

2. Peel the cucumbers, cut in half lengthwise, and scoop out the seeds with a spoon. Slice into large chunks.

3. Cut the root end off the scallions and discard. Trim the scallions to 5-inch lengths, measuring from the bulb end, and reserve some of the unused green tops to chop for garnish.

4. Place the slice of bread, broken into large chunks, in a food processor or blender and whirl on and off a few times to chop the bread into crumbs. Add the tomatoes, cucumber, scallions, and remaining ingredients to the workbowl of the processor and blend until everything is finely chopped.

5. Chill at least 4 hours so the soup is completely cold, and serve garnished with the reserved chopped green tops of the scallions.

Makes 6 servings

VARIATIONS

Cold Tomato Sauce

Add one more cup of tomato juice to the soup recipe, increasing the amount if necessary, to create a thick, spoonable consistency.

Bloody Mary

Add 3 more cups of tomato juice to the soup recipe and add vodka to taste. Garnish with a peeled, halved, and seeded cucumber cut into long fingers.

TRANSPORTATION TIP

Thoroughly chill the soup before packing up. To keep it cold, chill the thermos it will travel in with ice water for 15 to 30 minutes. When ready to leave, pour out the water and substitute the cold soup.

If possible, pack the thermos alongside other cold items, though it can be stored with loose supplies, like the cups or mugs and spoons.

Butternut Apple Soup

The promise of fall is in the air and the new crop of apples has made it to market along with winter squash. Pair the two in this golden soup, add a touch of curry for a little zest, and serve this hot from a thermos when the air begins to get a little nippy.

1 1/2 pounds butternut squash (1 small)
1 1/2 pounds Jonathan or Granny Smith apples (3 large)
3 cups water
2 teaspoons granulated sugar
Pinch of ground cloves
1/2 teaspoon salt
Freshly ground white pepper
1 teaspoon curry powder
1 cup heavy whipping cream

1. Cut the squash in half lengthwise and scoop out the seeds and fiber. Cut in half again, lengthwise, and pare off the outside shell. Cut the squash into cubes.

2. Quarter, core, and pare the apples. Cut them into cubes also.

3. Place the squash, apples, water, sugar, cloves, salt and pepper in a large saucepan or casserole. Bring to a boil, reduce heat, cover, and simmer 30 to 45 minutes or until the squash and apples are extremely soft and beginning to form a purée.

4. Purée the mixture (including the water) in a food processor or blender. The soup may be stored in the refrigerator at this point.

5. Before serving, stir together the squash-apple mixture, curry powder, and cream in a saucepan. Bring slowly to a simmer and taste for seasoning. Should the soup be too thick, add a little water.

Makes 6 servings

TRANSPORTATION TIP

Store this soup in the refrigerator until you're ready to go, then heat it to a simmer.

Pour the hot soup into a thermos that has been warmed with boiling water for 15 to 30 minutes. If there's room, pack it with other hot foods, though it may be kept separate.

And don't forget the bowls. Spoons are optional since this soup can also be sipped from a cup or mug.

Carrot and Leek Soup

As much as I want to love vichyssoise, it nevertheless reminds me of wallpaper paste. With the substitution of carrots, however, this soup takes on a new meaning, a friendly color and more substantial flavor, especially when uncluttered by the taste of chicken stock. Best of all, it's a snap to make, and good hot as well as cold.

½ pound carrots (4 medium)
1 pound leeks (2 medium)
4 cups water
½ teaspoon salt
½ cup heavy whipping cream

1. Peel the carrots and cut into 1-inch chunks.

2. Cut off the green tops of the leeks and discard. About 3 inches of the white bulb end will remain. Starting ½-inch above the root, slit each leek in half and fan out the layers under running water to rinse out any sand. Cut off the root end and discard. Chop the leek into 1-inch pieces.

3. Place the carrots and leeks in salted water in a large saucepan. Bring to a boil, reduce the heat, and simmer, uncovered, 40 to 45 minutes or until the vegetables are very tender.

4. Purée the mixture (including the water) in a blender or food processor until smooth. Add the whipping cream and whirl briefly. Taste and add more salt if necessary. Chill completely before serving or reheat if a hot soup is preferred.

Makes 6 servings

VARIATION

Watercress and Leek Soup

This tangy, green soup is the thinner, peppery version. To make it, replace the carrots with 1 bunch of watercress, trimmed of the woody stems. Cooking time will be reduced to about 30 minutes.

TRANSPORTATION TIP

Store this soup in the refrigerator until ready to leave, then heat it thoroughly if you want it to be served hot.

Temper the thermos with boiling or icy water, depending on whether the soup will be served hot or cold. Pour off the water and replace with the soup.

Pack it with other foods served at the same temperature. Or keep the thermos with items like cups and spoons, though spoons are optional here because this soup can be sipped from a mug.

Guacamole with Pistachios

The buttery taste and bright green color of the avocado matches beautifully with chopped pistachios in this version of the classic dip, which combines rich flavor and color with a bit of appealing crunch. The addition of scallions, tomato, lemon, and Tabasco make it a dip that goes equally well with homemade Cornmeal Soda Crackers (see page 114) or store-bought chips.

> *6 medium scallions*
> *1 ripe medium tomato*
> *3 ripe medium avocados*
> *¼ cup chopped pistachios, reserving 1 teaspoon*
>   *for garnish*
> *½ teaspoon grated lemon rind*
> *1 tablespoon fresh lemon juice*
> *Tabasco*
> *2 or 3 tablespoons sour cream*

1. Cut the root end off the scallions and discard. Now trim the scallions to 8-inch lengths, reserving some of the unused green tops to chop for garnish. Cut each scallion in half lengthwise and finely chop.

2. Cut the tomato in half crosswise, squeeze out the seeds, and finely chop.

3. Cut the avocados in half lengthwise, remove the pits, and scoop out the pulp with a spoon. Thoroughly mash the avocados in a bowl with a fork or purée through a potato ricer or in a food processor.

4. Combine the scallions, tomato, and avocados with the pistachios, lemon rind and lemon juice. Blend thoroughly and add salt and drops of Tabasco to taste.

5. Transfer to a serving dish. Stir the sour cream to a loose, spreadable consistency and completely coat the surface of the guacamole with it to insulate the mixture from air so the avocados won't turn brown. Garnish with chopped scallion greens and pistachios.

Makes 3 cups

TRANSPORTATION TIP

Thoroughly chill the guacamole in the refrigerator in a serving dish or storage container. One with sides and a lid works best.

Pack it with the other cold foods when you're ready to go. No utensils are required, though don't forget the crackers or chips.

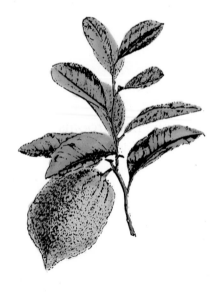

Rosy Marinated Mushrooms

These delicate, rosy-beige marinated mushrooms are out of the ordinary, mainly because of their cheerful good looks and marvelous taste. Serve these on a cupped lettuce leaf or, if you are planning a more elaborate picnic, pile them in individual soufflé dishes or Japanese tea cups.

1 pound tightly closed, fresh button mushrooms;
    small, bite-sized ones are best

Dressing:
    3 medium scallions, trimmed to 6-inch lengths
        measuring from the root, and cut in chunks
    1/3 cup red wine vinegar
    1/4 cup good-quality olive oil
    1/4 cup vegetable oil
    1/4 cup granulated sugar
    1/2 teaspoon dry mustard
    1/2 teaspoon salt

1. If necessary, wipe the mushrooms with a damp cloth to clean. Leave the mushrooms whole unless they are large enough to warrant cutting in half. Place in a container with a tight-fitting lid.

2. To make the dressing: Place the scallions and the remaining ingredients in a blender or food processor and mix until smoothly blended and the scallions are so finely chopped they're unnoticeable.

3. Pour the dressing over the mushrooms and stir or shake so all the mushrooms are mixed with the marinade. Let them rest in the covered dish in the refrigerator for 24 hours, stirring occasionally to redistribute the mushrooms in the marinade.

4. Mushrooms should be lifted out of the sauce at the end of that time, though they may remain in a covered dish in the refrigerator until serving.

Makes 6 servings

TRANSPORTATION TIP

Keep the chilled mushrooms in a storage container with a tight-fitting lid, remembering to lift them out of the marinade after 24 hours or before packing them with other cold foods when ready to leave.

For serving, take along small dishes or rinsed and dried lettuce-leaf cups stored in a plastic bag alongside other cold foods.

The mushrooms can be considered finger food, though forks or toothpicks are acceptable implements.

Gravlax with Sour Cream Mustard Sauce

When fresh salmon came only as a whole unit or cut into steaks, gravlax—the brine cured version of the smoked salmon—was tricky business. Since the steaks couldn't be used, it meant boning a salmon on your own or talking the person behind the fish counter into doing it for you. But with salmon fillets now an option, gravlax requires only the presence of mind to know that you need to let it rest for 48 hours before serving. It also helps to have a sharp knife to slice off thin, diagonal pieces, the gravlax trademark.

Salmon:
> *¹/₂ pound fresh salmon fillet*
> *2 tablespoons imported vodka*
> *1 rounded teaspoon coarse (kosher) salt*
> *1 rounded teaspoon granulated sugar*
> *Fresh dill weed*

Sour Cream Mustard Sauce:
> *¹/₂ cup sour cream*
> *¹/₂ teaspoon prepared mustard*
> *Pinch of salt*

1. Place the salmon, skin side down, in a glass or enameled baking pan. Pour the vodka over the fleshy side of the fish, sprinkle with salt and sugar, and cover completely with sprigs of dill weed.

2. Place a piece of plastic wrap on top of the salmon and weight it down with a heavy object. A smaller glass baking pan with a heavy object resting inside works well here.

3. Place the salmon in the refrigerator for 48 hours, letting it marinate and cure in the brine that will collect in this time.

4. To make the sour cream mustard sauce: Stir together the sour cream, mustard, and salt. Season to taste.

5. Scrape the dill and any remaining crystals of salt off the salmon, place on a cutting board, and slice thinly on the diagonal. Serve with sauce and thin toast triangles or Plain Soda Crackers (see page 115).

Makes 6 servings

TRANSPORTATION TIP

Keep the gravlax refrigerated until ready to pack, though lift it out of the brine at the end of 48 hours. It may be thinly sliced on the diagonal and placed on a serving plate before packing, but it's more fun to wrap up the fillet in aluminum foil and take it whole to the site so that guests can slice pieces themselves. In that case, bring a sharp knife, which should be thoroughly wrapped in napkins and carefully packed.

Pimiento Cheese

Kids of all ages like pimiento cheese. Not only does it go well when sandwiched between two slices of bread or mounded on a celery stick, but it also tastes elegant enough to spread on the most sophisticated cracker. This mixture keeps amazingly well in the refrigerator— but only if you hide it in the back so no one can find it.

6 ounces cream cheese, softened
12 ounces American cheese, grated (4 cups, loosely
 packed)
1/3 cup diced and drained pimientos
1/2 cup good-quality mayonnaise
2 tablespoons granulated sugar
Pinch of salt

1. Place the cream cheese in mixing bowl and stir until completely smooth. Mix in the grated American cheese and pimientos.

2. In a separate bowl, stir together the mayonnaise, sugar and salt until creamy and the grains of sugar are dissolved. Then thoroughly blend the mayonnaise into the cheese.

Makes 3 cups

TRANSPORTATION TIP

Refrigerate the pimiento cheese until you're ready to begin making sandwiches and packing up. If you plan to prepare the sandwiches at the picnic site, keep the spread in a covered storage container.

Whichever way you do it, this food gets packed with other cold items when ready to leave.

Remember to take a spreading knife or spoon if the sandwiches won't be made at home.

Spinach Puffs in Phyllo

Thin sheets of phyllo pastry, lightly brushed with butter and baked to crinkly perfection, make an impressive starter for any meal. Not only do these taste exceptionally fine, but everyone will assume you've been chained to the kitchen for hours making them. Looks surely can be deceiving. In fact, this recipe is simple enough for even an inexperienced phyllo dough baker to try. All you have to remember is to work at a steady pace so the sheets of pastry don't dry out.

10 sheets phyllo dough, normally available in boxes in the freezer case
4 tablespoons unsalted butter, melted
Filling:
1 package (10 ounces) frozen leaf spinach, completely thawed and squeezed dry using a strainer or the hands
3/4 cup walnuts
8 ounces cream cheese, softened
Salt
Diced pimiento or red bell pepper (35 small pieces), for garnish

1. If the phyllo dough is frozen, thaw according to directions on the package. Note that this recipe will use approximately half a box of pastry.

2. Unwrap the dough and lay out flat on a work surface, laying sheets of plastic wrap over the dough to keep it from drying out. Have the butter and a pastry brush or feather nearby.

3. Lift off one sheet of dough from the stack and place on a clean surface. Brush a little butter on the underside of the dough at the four corners to keep this sheet from sliding around the counter. Then ever so lightly brush the top side of the dough with a thin glaze of butter.

4. Lift off another sheet of dough from the stack, place it directly on top of the first buttered sheet and smooth it out. Lightly brush this with butter also. Continue stacking and buttering until there are a total of 10 sheets of phyllo dough.

5. Use a ruler to mark off 2½-inch squares. This phyllo rectangle should make 7 squares one way and 5 the other with a little extra dough left over. Use a sharp knife or a pastry wheel to completely cut through the 35 squares that have been marked.

6. Rewrap and store the unused phyllo dough. Cover the completed squares with plastic wrap until ready to use.

7. Make the filling now or prepare it ahead of time while the dough is defrosting: Place the thawed and squeezed-dry spinach in a blender or food processor along with the walnuts and finely chop. Add the softened cream cheese and a pinch of salt and whirl until completely blended. Taste and add more salt, if necessary.

8. Heat the oven to 375° F. Place squares of phyllo dough in the cups of two 12-cup miniature muffin tins, pushing in the center to create indentations and leaving the four corners folded over the edge of each cup.

9. Fill each cup with a teaspoon of the spinach filling. Garnish with a small piece of pimiento or chopped red bell pepper. Bake in the hot oven 12 to 15 minutes until the spinach has puffed up and the edges of the pastry are golden brown. Cool slightly and lift the pastry cups out onto a wire rack until serving time. Continue to fill the muffin tray and bake the remaining squares.

Makes 35 appetizers

Ham and Cheese Puffs in Phyllo

Instead of the spinach filling, substitute a mixture made by blending together:

8 ounces (2 cups, loosely packed) ground or finely chopped ham

8 ounces (2 cups, loosely packed) finely shredded mild cheddar cheese

1/2 teaspoon dry mustard

Pinch of cayenne pepper

TRANSPORTATION TIP

The puffs can be kept in the refrigerator for two or three days in a covered container. Separate the layers of puffs with wax paper so they don't stick together and pack nearby other cold foods in an insulated cooler. Bring them to room temperature before serving.

As an alternative, wrap the puffs in aluminum foil and place in an oven heated to 350° F. for about 15 minutes to warm up. Then store them with the hot foods.

No utensils are necessary with this finger food though you might want to take along a serving plate for a more elegant presentation at the picnic site.

ENTRÉES

APPLE-GLAZED PORK TENDERLOIN

BARBECUED WHOLE PORK TENDERLOIN

BABY BACK RIBS WITH BARBECUE SAUCE

GRILLED BABY BACK RIBS

ALMOND FRIED CHICKEN

CURRIED CHICKEN SALAD WITH GRAPES

ROASTED CHICKEN

CHICKEN ROASTED ON A GRILL

CHILI MOLÉ

FLANK STEAK FLORENTINE

GRILLED LEG OF LAMB

GRILLED LAMB ON A STICK

POACHED TUNA WITH CUCUMBER SAUCE

CUCUMBER SOUP

STUDY IN RED SHRIMP SALAD

SALMON TERRINE WITH BAY SCALLOPS

CREAMY CORKSCREW PASTA WITH

SCALLOPS AND VEGETABLES

CAESAR PASTA SALAD WITH TUNA

ONION AND RICOTTA PIE

JARLSBERG AND POTATO PIE

Apple-Glazed Pork Tenderloin

The marinade for this tenderloin is good enough to drink, and it adds a surprisingly complex and spicy flavor to the tenderloin as well. Apples, of course, are a natural pairing with pork, just as cider mulls beautifully with bourbon, sugar, and cinnamon. This delicate blend is the result. Thin slices of tenderloin are perfect for sandwiches; thicker slices can be served alone.

1 or 2 whole pork tenderloins (each about 3/4 pound)

Marinade:
1/2 cup sour mash whiskey
1/2 cup unfiltered apple cider
1/4 cup firmly packed brown sugar
1/8 teaspoon ground cinnamon
Barbecue Sauce

1. Place the pork tenderloin in a glass or enameled low-sided baking dish.

2. Thoroughly mix the whiskey, cider, brown sugar, and cinnamon and pour over the tenderloin. Cover the dish with plastic wrap and refrigerate 8 hours or more. If possible, turn the tenderloin over several times during this time.

3. Heat the oven to 325° F. Place the tenderloin, still resting in the marinade, in the hot oven and cook 1 hour and 15 minutes or until the internal temperature of the meat is 170° F. Every 15 or 20 minutes, brush the tenderloin with the gradually reducing marinade.

Once the tenderloin is done, let it stand out of the oven 10 to 15 minutes before carving. Serve with barbecue sauce.

Makes 4 to 10 servings, depending on number of tenderloins cooked and whether used alone or in sandwiches

VARIATION

Barbecued Whole Pork Tenderloin

Marinate the tenderloin as directed, but cook over a low fire on a charcoal grill, turning every 15 minutes and basting. Barbecue with the lid closed about 1½ hours or until the meat reaches an internal temperature of 170° F.

TRANSPORTATION TIP

If you are cooking a day or two ahead of time, store the tenderloin in the refrigerator. If serving cool, take it to the picnic site stored with the cold foods. If serving warm, heat the foil-wrapped tenderloin in a 350° F. oven 15 to 20 minutes to take the chill off and pack with the hot foods.

The sliced tenderloin can be cut ahead of time, reassembled as a long cylinder and wrapped in foil. Alternatively, it can be carried whole—wrapped in foil—and sliced at the picnic site. In that case be sure to bring along a carefully wrapped carving knife.

If you are cooking at the picnic site, don't forget the charcoal, lighter fluid, and grill.

Baby Back Ribs with Barbecue Sauce

Baby back ribs are one of the specialty cuts of pork. Being closest to the backbone and running down the loin, they are meatier and more tender than their country or sparerib cousins and consequently command a higher price. It's worth it, however, since you'll have to take along fewer of them—and on a picnic that is a decided advantage.

> *Salt*
> *Pinch of ground sage*
> *4¹/₂ to 5 pounds pork baby back ribs*

Barbecue Sauce:
> *2 tablespoons vegetable oil*
> *3 tablespoons grated onion*
> *1 can (10³/₄ ounces) tomato purée*
> *¹/₃ cup Worcestershire sauce*
> *¹/₃ cup honey*
> *3 tablespoons red wine vinegar*
> *1 teaspoon dry mustard*
> *Pinch of cayenne pepper*
> *Salt and freshly ground black pepper*

1. Bring a large pot of salted water to a boil. Add the sage and ribs and bring back to a boil. Reduce the heat and let the ribs simmer 5 minutes. Drain off the water and, if you're going to do this ahead of time, store the meat in the refrigerator.

2. To make the barbecue sauce: Place the vegetable oil in a saucepan over medium-low heat. Add the onion and cook gently until the onion is tender and light yellow.

3. Add the tomato purée, Worcestershire sauce, honey, vinegar, and mustard and bring to a simmer over medium heat. Taste and season with cayenne and salt and black pepper. The sauce may be made ahead and refrigerated.

4. To finish cooking the ribs: Heat the oven to 350° F. Place the ribs in a low roasting pan and lightly baste the top side with sauce. Cook in the oven about 1 hour, turning the ribs and lightly basting every 10 to 15 minutes.

Makes 6 servings

Note: For smaller quantities, buy fewer ribs (figuring ³/₄ pound per person), but make the same amount of sauce, since it keeps well in the refrigerator and can be used with other recipes.

VARIATION

Grilled Baby Back Ribs

Cook the ribs in water as directed, but finish cooking over a low fire on a charcoal grill, turning every 15 minutes. Start basting with the barbeque sauce after 30 minutes. Total cooking time is about 60 minutes.

TRANSPORTATION TIP

The ribs can be served warm or cold. If they're cooked ahead of time, store them in the refrigerator, wrapped in foil or placed in a covered container. If you are serving them cold, transport them to the picnic stored with the cold foods. If you prefer them warm, heat the foil-wrapped ribs in a 350° F. oven 15 or 20 minutes to take the chill off. In that case, pack with the hot foods.

Either cut the ribs into individual pieces before packing or take along a sharp, carefully wrapped knife and cut them on site.

Any extra sauce can be stored in a covered container and carried along also. Chill or heat it, depending on your preference, and store either as a hot or cold item. Take along a spoon for serving the sauce and plenty of paper napkins and moist packaged towels for cleaning up after eating this finger food.

If planning to cook on the spot, don't forget the grill, charcoal, and lighter fluid.

Almond Fried Chicken

Fried chicken is a picnic staple. Not only is it tasty, but it also travels well, being as good cold as it is hot from the frying pan. Here, boneless breasts are coated with finely chopped almonds to add a nutty flavor to an old-fashioned favorite.

6 boned, skinned chicken breast halves (about 1 1/2 pounds)
1/3 cup all-purpose flour
1/8 teaspoon salt
1 egg
3 tablespoons heavy whipping cream
1 cup almonds, finely chopped
1 cup fresh bread crumbs (2 slices finely chopped or grated)
4 tablespoons unsalted butter
4 tablespoons peanut oil

1. The chicken breasts are coated in a three-step process easily accomplished if each element is handy in a low-sided dish, like a cake pan. Combine the flour and salt in one pan, beat the egg with the whipping cream in another and mix the almonds and bread crumbs in a third. Have a wire cooking rack ready to hold the breaded chicken before and after frying.

2. Place two breast halves at a time in the flour. Dust both sides of the chicken, pounding in the flour so it sticks to the meat. The breast will flatten out in the process.

3. Shake off any excess flour and drop the breasts in the egg mixture, turning over to moisten both sides.

4. Lift the chicken out of the liquid and place in the almond bread crumbs. Again, pound in this mixture on both sides before placing the breasts on the wire rack. Repeat the process with the remaining pieces.

5. Heat two tablespoons of both the butter and oil in a heavy frying pan over medium-high heat. When this is hot, add half of the breasts (do not crowd them in the pan) and sauté until lightly golden. Then turn the meat and cook the other side. Now reduce the heat to medium, turn the chicken back to the original side and cook until golden brown. Turn the breasts again and finish cooking. Total time will be about 20 minutes. Repeat the process with the remaining breasts, adding more butter and oil as necessary. (Alternatively, cook in two frying pans.) Cool briefly on the wire rack before refrigerating.

Makes 6 servings

TRANSPORTATION TIP

If making several hours or a day ahead of time, refrigerate the chicken wrapped in foil or stored in a covered container. Take it to the picnic with the other cold foods.

While this food could be eaten with a knife and fork, it's more in the spirit of outdoor dining to serve it as a finger food.

Curried Chicken Salad with Grapes

Cool, juicy, and colorful grapes combine with toasty almonds and hot, golden curry to make this chicken salad flavorful and refreshing. It's perfect for a summer day and so attractive you won't want to hide it between slices of bread. Serve it instead on a leaf of Bibb lettuce or tucked up against slices of tomato.

> *4 cups chicken stock*
> *4 boned, skinned chicken breasts (about 1 pound)*
> *¼ cup slivered almonds*
> *½ cup good-quality mayonnaise*
> *3 tablespoons heavy whipping cream*
> *½ teaspoon curry powder*
> *Salt or granulated sugar*
> *⅔ cup seedless grapes (if possible, mixed half red, half green*

1. Bring the chicken stock to a boil in a large saucepan and add the chicken breasts. Let the stock come back to a simmer, lower the heat, and cook gently for 20 to 25 minutes, partially covered. Lift the breasts out of the stock and cool. Save the stock for another use.

2. Scatter the almonds on a baking sheet and lightly toast for 6 to 8 minutes in an oven heated to 325° F.

3. Thoroughly blend the mayonnaise, whipping cream, and curry powder and season to taste with salt or sugar.

4. To assemble: Cut the cooled breasts into large chunks. Place the chicken, almonds, and grapes in a mixing bowl. Add as much of the dressing as necessary to reach a consistency you like.

Makes 6 servings

TRANSPORTATION TIP

Refrigerate the chicken salad in a covered container until ready to go and then pack it with the other cold foods. If serving with lettuce cups, be sure the leaves are rinsed, dried, and placed in a sealed plastic bag or a covered container before packing them with the cold foods. If serving with slices of tomato, you can cut these ahead of time, storing them in a covered container or wrapped in foil. Or simply take along a whole tomato and a sharp knife, carefully wrapped and packed.

Forks are in order here.

Roasted Chicken

Somewhere along the line, whole chickens went out of vogue, displaced by the more fashionable portioned parts now found in the meat case of the grocery store. It's unfortunate, because nothing is easier to cook than a roasted whole chicken, and little else offers such diversity while being conveniently packaged as a single unit. On top of that, it travels well and tastes grand at outdoor eating temperatures.

2 chickens, each weighing 3¹/₂ to 4 pounds
¹/₄ cup Dijon mustard
Salt
1 teaspoon paprika
1 tablespoon fresh tarragon or 1 teaspoon dried
    tarragon

1. Heat the oven to 400° F. Dry chickens inside and out with paper toweling. Tie the legs together with kitchen twine and fold the tips of the wings back and under the chickens.

2. Cover the chickens with a thick layer of Dijon mustard. Then sprinkle all over with salt, paprika, and tarragon.

3. Place the chickens in a roasting pan and slide into the hot oven. Immediately turn the heat down to 375° F. Roast a total of 1¹/₂ hours, basting with any accumulating juices after the first half hour of cooking and then every 20 minutes. The chickens are done when the legs move easily in their sockets. As an alternative test, deeply prick the thickest part of the thigh; the juice that flows out should be clear.

4. Remove the chickens from the roasting pan and cool.

Makes 6 servings

Chicken Roasted on a Grill

Cut down one side and then the other of the backbone of the chickens with poultry shears or a heavy knife. Discard the backbone and lay the bird, skin side down, on a work surface with the neck end closest to you. Use a sharp knife to cut through the small white piece of cartilage that lies between the neck and the keel bone that runs down the center of the breast. Bend back both halves of the chickens to pop up the keel bone. Carefully cut it out and discard. Cook on a grill over hot embers for 30 to 45 minutes, until the juices run clear. Turn the meat three or four times while it is roasting.

TRANSPORTATION TIP

If you are making the chicken several hours or a day ahead of time, wrap it in foil and refrigerate. When ready to go, pack it with the other cold foods. Or wrap it directly from the oven and tuck it in with the hot items.

You have a choice of either cutting it up beforehand or taking along a sharp knife or poultry shears to carve it on the spot.

Chili Molé

Not exactly the purist's approach to chili, this version nevertheless has a marvelous flavor and deep, rich, inviting color. If you don't mention it, no one will be the wiser that you've added the chocolate and raisins. Your guests will wonder, however, what makes it taste so good. I've stuck by the addition of raisins ever since accidently adding them many years ago while cleaning out the pantry. The chocolate crept in only recently.

2 pounds ground chuck
2 medium yellow onions, diced
2 medium garlic cloves, minced
¼ cup all-purpose flour
⅔ cup dark raisins, chopped
2 cans (28 ounces each) whole peeled tomatoes
2 cans (10¾ ounces each) tomato purée
2 cans (16 ounces each) red beans, (such as kidney beans) drained
2 cans (4 ounces each) diced green chilies, drained, or 2 fresh green chilies, seeded and diced
1 cup water
2 ounces unsweetened chocolate
4 teaspoons dried oregano
2 teaspoons chili powder
2 teaspoons ground cumin
Cayenne pepper
Salt and freshly ground black pepper
Garnish:
1 cup chopped red onion
1 cup grated cheddar cheese

1. Crumble the ground beef into a large saucepan and brown it, uncovered, over medium-high heat until some fat accumulates in the bottom of the pan. Stir occasionally.

2. Add the onion and garlic and cook until the onion is tender and the meat is thoroughly cooked. Stir frequently so the onions and garlic don't burn.

3. Sprinkle the flour over this mixture and stir it around for 3 or 4 minutes until no clumps remain and the flour has cooked briefly.

4. Now add the raisins, tomatoes, tomato purée, beans, chilies and water. Blend thoroughly and bring to a simmer. Lower the heat, stir in the chocolate and remaining seasonings, and cook—barely bubbling—for 20 to 30 minutes. The chili may now be refrigerated. Slowly bring it back to a boil before packing in a thermos to keep it hot.

Serve individual portions topped with chopped red onion and grated cheddar cheese.

Makes 6 hearty servings

TRANSPORTATION TIP

Store the chili and each garnish in separate containers in the refrigerator until ready to use.

Heat the chili thoroughly before transferring it to a thermos that has been tempered with boiling water. If possible, pack it with other hot foods, but put the onions and cheese with the cold items.

Take serving spoons for the garnishes and soup spoons or tablespoons for the chili.

Flank Steak Florentine

Flank steak may not be the most tender cut of beef, but it surely is one of the tastiest. This recipe pairs the substantial taste of beef rolled around the equally forceful flavor of spinach. Sliced thin, it is marvelous on a sandwich (made from a Pullman Loaf, page 110); cut in thicker pieces, it can be served with a cold, chunky tomato sauce (see Cold Tomato Sauce, page 65) for a knife-and-fork presentation.

1 flank steak (about 3¹/₂ pounds)
1 bunch fresh spinach (³/₄ to 1 pound)
2 tablespoons unsalted butter
2 large shallots, diced (¹/₄ cup)
Salt and freshly ground black pepper
Freshly grated nutmeg

1. Pound the flank steak with a heavy, smooth-surfaced object (like a small iron skillet or smooth meat mallet) to flatten it and break down some of the muscle tissue for easier rolling. Work the meat into a rectangle as much as possible.

2. Trim the spinach and rinse it in several changes of water to wash off any sand. There should be approximately 4 cups of lightly packed leaves. Steam the spinach over boiling water 2 or 3 minutes, just enough so it becomes limp. Drain off any water.

3. Heat the oven to 450° F.

4. Place 1 tablespoon of butter in a frying pan over low heat. Add the shallots and cook until they become limp and have absorbed the butter.

5. Spread the shallots over the flank steak, which has been lightly seasoned with salt and pepper. Lay the spinach on top, covering the whole surface, and season it with a little nutmeg. Roll up the meat and spinach, starting at the short end of the steak. Tie in four places with kitchen twine.

6. Melt the remaining 1 tablespoon butter and brush the outside of the roll with it. Again, lightly season with salt and pepper. Place the flank steak, seam side down, on a rack in a roasting pan and put in the hot oven. Immediately lower the heat to 275° F. and cook 1 hour 15 minutes for a slightly pink steak or 1 hour 30 minutes for well-done meat. Remove from the roasting pan and cool.

Makes 6 servings

TRANSPORTATION TIP

Refrigerate the rolled flank steak wrapped in foil and pack it with the other cold foods.

The flank steak may be sliced thick or thin, depending on how it's to be used, and rewrapped before leaving the house. However, it can also be transported whole, and carving can be done at the picnic site. In that case remember to take along a sharp knife. If serving thick slices, take along knives and forks.

Grilled Leg of Lamb

Fortunately, lamb is no longer a seasonal item. What used to be considered a spring delicacy is now available all through the year. And though the leg is most often served at home as a whole roast, it's also possible to remove the bone, flatten the leg, and take it on a picnic to cook on the grill. Have the butcher remove the bone for you, or do it yourself, following the directions below.

For even quicker cooking and easier serving, cut the major sections of the boned leg into thin slices and thread the meat on bamboo skewers before grilling.

1 leg of lamb, rump half (3 to 3¹/₂ pounds)
Marinade:
2 cups pineapple juice
¹/₂ cup fresh lemon juice (2 lemons)
¹/₂ cup mild-flavored honey
3 large garlic cloves, peeled and flattened
1 teaspoon ground ginger
1 teaspoon dry mustard
1 teaspoon salt

1. To butterfly the leg of lamb: Start by removing the long, flat aitchbone at the wide, rump end of this cut. Use a sharp boning or paring knife to make short incisions around the bone, cutting down into the meat—following the bone—until it is completely exposed. Sever the tendon connections at the socket where the aitchbone joins the leg bone and remove the aitchbone completely. With the fatty side of the leg on the work surface, cut through the natural muscle division, making an incision the length of the leg bone. Cut along both sides of the bone and then underneath to lift it out. Do not cut completely through the meat or there won't be anything to hold the separate muscles together.

2. To make the marinade: Combine all the ingredients in a large glass or enameled baking pan.

3. Place the meat in the marinade and refrigerate at least 24 hours, turning it over from time to time so both sides rest in the liquid.

4. Cook the leg over hot embers on a charcoal grill for about 45 minutes, or until the meat reaches an internal temperature of 135° F. for medium-rare or 140° F. for medium. Turn the meat over every 10 minutes so both sides cook evenly. Remove from the heat and let stand 10 minutes before carving.

Makes 10 to 12 servings

VARIATION

Grilled Lamb on a Stick

Remove the aitchbone and leg bone as described above. Then separate the leg into its major muscle divisions. Place the meat in the freezer for 45 to 60 minutes or until it becomes fully chilled and firm, but not frozen. Thinly cut each section of meat into ³/₈-inch slices. Thread the meat onto bamboo skewers, weaving it in and out. Several pieces of meat can be placed on each stick. Marinate the skewered lamb at least 12 hours before grilling. Cooking time will be 5 to 10 minutes.

TRANSPORTATION TIP

Remove the lamb, either butterflied or on skewers, from the marinade before wrapping in foil or storing in a covered container for picnic portability. Pack it with other cold foods.

If serving the leg whole, take along a sharp knife. Be sure it is carefully wrapped and packed.

Naturally, you'll also remember the charcoal, lighter fluid, and grill.

Poached Tuna with Cucumber Sauce

Now that tuna is out of the can and in the seafood case, it's beginning to rival salmon as an easy-to-fix, cook-it-almost-any-way fresh fish. Here it's poached, but it could just as easily be grilled over a low fire. As with all fish, the secret is to cook it just until it flakes. Some would suggest that even this is too long, and that fish should be served medium-rare. One thing is certain, however. Cooking it beyond the flaking stage toughens the fish considerably. So beware.

To add a delicate shade to the deep color of the tuna, serve it with the pale green cucumber sauce flecked with bright dill and golden raisins. By adding more whipping cream, this sauce could also become a refreshing soup.

1 lemon
10 cups water
1 celery rib, diced
4 scallions, trimmed, or half a small onion, diced
1 tablespoon fresh dill or 1 teaspoon dried
Salt and 8 peppercorns, cracked
6 small fresh tuna steaks or fillets, each weighing
    about ¼ pound
Cucumber Sauce:
1 medium cucumber
½ cup plain yogurt
2 tablespoons heavy whipping cream
2 tablespoons golden raisins
1 tablespoon fresh dill or 1 teaspoon dried
Salt

1. Cut the lemon in half, squeeze the juice and add both lemon and juice to the water in a large saucepan. Bring to a boil along with the celery, onion, dill, salt, and peppercorns. Reduce the heat and simmer 30 minutes before lifting out the vegetables and seasonings, leaving the flavored water in the saucepan.

2. When this liquid is once again bubbling, add the tuna fillets, bring the liquid back to a simmer, and poach over low heat 3 or 4 minutes until the tuna is opaque and layers can be flaked off with a fork. Lift out and cool.

3. To make the cucumber sauce: Peel the cucumber, cut off the ends and cut in half lengthwise, scooping out the seeds with a spoon. Cut into chunks and place in a food processor or blender.

4. Add the yogurt, cream, raisins, dill and salt and chop just until the sauce is slightly chunky. Serve the sauce over the tuna, garnished with a tiny sprig of dill.

Makes 6 servings; sauce makes 1½ cups

VARIATION

Cucumber Soup

Add 2 to 4 tablespoons more heavy whipping cream to the mixture in the blender. Makes 2 or 3 servings of soup.

TRANSPORTATION TIP

Refrigerate the poached fish wrapped in foil or tucked in a covered container until ready to pack for the picnic. This can be done up to a day in advance. Then pack it with the other cold foods.

The sauce should also be refrigerated until ready to go. Put it in a container with a tight-fitting lid so it doesn't slosh about and leak in transit. It, too, is packed with cold foods and requires a spoon for serving.

The tuna fillets can be cut with a fork, though it never hurts to bring along knives.

Study in Red Shrimp Salad

The radishes were originally added to this shrimp salad as a way of extending it—grated radishes mixed with mayonnaise used to be considered the poor person's substitute for shellfish salad. Then having combined the two reds, it seemed appropriate to add a third with the red pepper. The flavors blend as beautifully as do the colors.

> *1¹/₂ pounds cooked and peeled shrimp, diced in large chunks*
> *1 large red bell pepper, seeded and diced (1¹/₂ cups)*
> *18 medium red radishes, trimmed and diced (1¹/₂ cups)*
> *1 small garlic clove, peeled and minced*
> *³/₄ cup good-quality mayonnaise*

1. Toss the shrimp, red pepper, and radishes together in a mixing bowl.

2. Blend the garlic with the mayonnaise and stir this into the shrimp mixture. Chill thoroughly.

Makes 6 servings.

TRANSPORTATION TIP

Make this salad up to a day ahead of time and chill it in the refrigerator before packing. It goes best in a container with a tight-fitting lid so the sauce—as well as the wonderful smell of garlic—is trapped. Pack it along with the other cold foods, remembering a spoon for serving.

Salmon Terrine with Bay Scallops

In the fifties this sort of dish would have been called a salmon loaf. It would have appeared without the bay scallops in the middle and capers would not have been used in the seasoning. Other than that, the principle is pretty much the same, and the taste is equally good, if slightly more complex for today's more adventurous palate.

1 pound fresh salmon, skin and bones (if any)
*   removed and cut into chunks*
1/2 cup fresh bread crumbs (1 slice finely chopped
*   or grated)*
1/2 cup finely chopped red onion
2 tablespoons heavy whipping cream
1 tablespoon capers, drained
1 tablespoon fresh dill, reserving a sprig for
*   garnish, or 1/2 teaspoon dried*
Salt and freshly ground black pepper
1/4 pound bay scallops, dusted with flour and salt

1. Butter a 2-cup terrine or loaf pan. Heat the oven to 250° F.

2. Place all the ingredients except the bay scallops in a blender or food processor and pulse on and off until the mixture is finely chopped.

3. Place half of this purée in the buttered terrine. Put the dusted scallops in a single layer over this. Pack the remaining salmon on top of the scallops and smooth out the surface. Decorate with a sprig of dill.

4. Bake for 1 hour or until the edge of the loaf begins to pull away from the baking container. This may be served warm or cold from the terrine or pan.

Makes 6 servings

TRANSPORTATION TIP

If cooking this just before leaving, pack it with the warm foods, leaving it in the terrine. If making it the day before the picnic, store it—mold and all—in the refrigerator until ready to go. At that point pack it with the cold foods, covered with foil.

    This terrine needs to be cut with a knife, and it also helps to have a pie server to ease it out.

Creamy Corkscrew Pasta with Scallops and Vegetables

The soft green and orange of the colored pasta blend beautifully with the matchsticks of carrots and celery found in this dish. Originally developed as a hot entree—minus the pasta—I found it tastes equally good at room temperature. However, since it nearly solidifies in the refrigerator, be sure to let it warm up a bit before serving.

> 2 cups dry, mixed-color corkscrew (rotini or twist)
>   pasta
> Salt
> 1 teaspoon plus 1 tablespoon vegetable oil
> l large carrot
> 1 celery rib
> 1 teaspoon fresh lemon juice
> ¼ cup water
> 1 pound bay scallops
> 1 cup heavy whipping cream
> 1 teaspoon Dijon mustard

1. Cook the pasta according to the directions on the package in a large pot of boiling, salted water. When the pasta is al dente, drain it and toss with 1 teaspoon vegetable oil.

2. While this is going on, cut the peeled carrot into 1- to 1½-inch lengths. Stand the carrots on the cut end and slice into strips ⅛-inch thick. Stack the strips and cut lengthwise into matchstick-sized pieces.

3. Cut the celery into 1- to 1½-inch lengths. Cut lengthwise into matchstick-sized pieces.

4. Place 1 tablespoon of oil in a frying pan over low heat and add the carrots and celery. Cook gently until the vegetables are limp but still crunchy.

5. Add the lemon juice, water, and salt to taste. Cover and simmer 3 or 4 minutes. Add the scallops and cover again. Simmer 2 to 3 minutes or just until the scallops are opaque. Use a slotted spoon to lift out the vegetables and seafood.

6. Blend the whipping cream and mustard into the juice remaining in the frying pan. Reduce this mixture for 3 or 4 minutes over medium heat, stirring occasionally, until it lightly coats a spoon. Return the vegetables and scallops to the pan and remove from the heat. Stir occasionally while the sauce is cooling. When the sauce is lukewarm, toss in the pasta and stir gently to coat it evenly before transferring the mixture to a serving dish. This may be refrigerated, but bring it back to room temperature before serving.

Makes 6 servings

TRANSPORTATION TIP

This recipe works best if it hasn't been held too long in the refrigerator. Or if it's been made a day in advance, be sure to let it warm up at least 20 minutes before serving so that the sauce has a chance to loosen.

Keep it in a covered container and have a serving spoon handy.

Caesar Pasta Salad with Tuna

If you like lemon and garlic, you're going to love this Caesar salad dressing. If any dressing is left over, try drizzling it over some romaine lettuce with a little anchovy and Parmesan cheese tossed in as well. Here, however, it is combined with canned tuna, that ever popular pantry staple and bedrock of sandwich making.

> 3 cups mixed-color small tube pasta like penne or
>   mostaccioli
> Salt
> 1 teaspoon vegetable oil
> 2 cans (each 6½ ounces) solid white tuna packed
>   in water
> ¾ cup finely and freshly grated Parmesan cheese
> 12 cherry tomatoes, quartered into wedges

Dressing:

> 1 egg
> 3 tablespoons fresh lemon juice
> 1½ teaspoons Dijon mustard
> 1 small garlic clove, peeled, trimmed, and
>   flattened
> Salt and freshly ground pepper
> ¼ cup vegetable oil
> ⅓ cup olive oil

1. Cook the pasta in a large quantity of boiling, salted water according to the directions on the package. When the pasta is al dente, drain and toss with the vegetable oil.

2. Thoroughly drain the tuna, firmly pressing the lid against the tuna in the can and pouring off all the water. Use a fork to flake off good-sized pieces of tuna into a large mixing bowl. Add the cooled pasta, cheese, and tomatoes and toss to mix thoroughly.

3. To make the dressing: Place the egg, lemon juice, mustard, garlic, and salt and pepper in a blender or food processor. Mix thoroughly. Then, with the motor running, slowly add the vegetable and olive oils in a thin stream. Pour ⅔ cup of this dressing over the pasta salad and carefully mix to blend. Add more sauce, if necessary.

Makes 6 servings

TRANSPORTATION TIP

Refrigerate the finished dish in a covered container, packing it with the other cold foods when ready to leave the house. It shouldn't be eaten icy cold, so take it out of the cooler 10 or 15 minutes before serving.

Remember to bring along a spoon for dishing up this entrée, which requires a fork.

Onion and Ricotta Pie

For those who prefer a minimalist, no-anxiety pie crust, this onion-ricotta blend rests atop a simple, no-roll, soda cracker base. Since it's baked in a springform pan, there's also no need to worry about crimping the edges.

Given the simple preparation and the unusual, flavorful taste, you'll find this an item you'll want to use again and again.

Crust:
> *36 small soda cracker squares, finely crushed in a*
> *blender or food processor (1½ cups)*
> *2 tablespoons granulated sugar*
> *4 tablespoons unsalted butter, melted*

Filling:
> *3 tablespoons peanut oil*
> *1 pound yellow onions (2 medium, peeled and cut*
> *in half through the root end and sliced*
> *¼-inch thick)*
> *4 tablespoons unsalted butter, softened*
> *1 container (16 ounces) whole-milk ricotta cheese*
> *3 eggs, beaten until frothy*

Topping:
> *1 tablespoon unsalted butter, softened*
> *1 cup fresh bread crumbs (2 slices finely chopped*
> *or grated)*
> *¼ cup, loosely packed, finely chopped fresh*
> *parsley*

1. Heat the oven to 400° F.

2. To make the crust: Place the crushed soda crackers and sugar in a mixing bowl. Pour over the melted butter and toss the mixture to moisten the crumbs. Scatter the mixture in the bottom of a 9-inch springform pan and pack down until a solid layer of crust has been formed. Bake for about 6 minutes, or until set and just beginning to color. Cool.

3. To make the filling and topping: Place the peanut oil in a large frying pan over medium-low heat. Add the sliced onions, cover, and cook gently 20 to 30 minutes. Stir often so none of the onions burn and remove from the heat when they are tender and golden.

4. Meanwhile, lower the oven to 325° F. Cream 4 tablespoons of butter and then beat in the ricotta cheese. Gradually stir in the thoroughly beaten eggs and set aside.

5. In another bowl, cream 1 tablespoon of butter and mix in the bread crumbs and parsley. The crumbs should be slightly moist.

6. Spread the cooked onions over the crust in the springform pan. Pour the ricotta-egg mixture over this. Scatter the bread crumbs over the surface and smooth out.

7. Bake 55 to 60 minutes, or until the top has puffed up and set. Cool and use a knife to loosen the edge of the pie from the pan before removing the ring and cutting. Slip the ring back in place for easy transporting.

Makes 6 servings

TRANSPORTATION TIP

You can prepare this dish ahead of time and store it in the refrigerator or bake it just before leaving. It can also be cut once it's slightly cool or packed whole. In the latter case, remember to bring a knife and pie server.

The pie—still in the springform pan—should be covered with aluminum foil and packed at the top of either the hot or cold foods, depending on how long it has been out of the oven.

This pie is best served with forks.

Jarlsberg and Potato Pie

This hearty potato-cheese pie is a perfect entrée to serve on a cool spring or fall day when you plan on taking a long hike before sitting down to eat. Though vaguely reminiscent of scalloped potatoes, the nutlike flavor of the Jarlsberg gives this dish a more robust and substantial character.

Pastry:

> *1¼ cups all-purpose or pastry flour*
> *½ teaspoon salt*
> *⅓ cup solid vegetable shortening*
> *1 egg*
> *2 teaspoons ice-cold water (optional)*

Filling:

> *1½ pounds russet potatoes (3 small, each 3 to 3½ inches long)*
> *6 ounces Jarlsberg cheese, grated (1½ cups lightly packed)*
> *1 medium garlic clove, minced*
> *1 cup heavy whipping cream*
> *¼ teaspoon salt*
> *Freshly ground black pepper*
> *16 thin slices smoked Polish sausage*

1. To make the pastry: Place the flour and salt in a mixing bowl. Add the shortening and use a fork or pastry blender to break it up into chunks about the size of small peas. Do not cut the fat into particles that are too fine. Lightly beat the egg and gradually add it to the flour, stirring, tossing, and lightly pressing the particles together to moisten evenly. Add the water, if necessary, to be able to work the mixture into a dough. Shape into a flattened round, wrap in wax paper, and refrigerate at least 20 minutes before rolling out.

2. To make the filling: Place the potatoes in salted water and bring to a boil. Partially cover and cook 20 to 30 minutes or just until a sharp knife can be inserted easily into the vegetable. Drain and place under cold running water. When cool, peel and coarsely grate.

3. To finish the pastry: Lightly flour both sides of the pie dough, as well as the work surface. Roll out the pastry to a ¹⁄₁₆- to ⅛-inch thick circle. Turn occasionally to be sure the dough isn't sticking. Gently fold the dough in quarters and unfold in a 9-inch pan, easing the dough down the sides. Trim the dough so it hangs over the rim by 1 inch. Fold the overhang up under the dough on the rim to form a double-walled crust and crimp. Heat the oven to 400° F.

4. To fill the pie: Scatter half the grated potatoes over the bottom of the pie pastry. Scatter half the grated cheese and all the minced garlic over this. Layer with the remaining potatoes and cheese. Pour the whipping cream, seasoned with salt and pepper, over everything. Garnish the edge of the filling with a ring of the sausage slices.

5. Bake in the hot oven for 30 to 40 minutes or until the cream is bubbling and the top is golden. Let stand 10 or 15 minutes before slicing.

Makes 6 servings

VARIATION

As an alternative, the crust may be made in a food processor by following these instructions:

1. Place the flour, salt and shortening in the bowl of a food processor fitted with a steel blade. Pulse the machine on and off 4 to 6 times until the pieces of fat are about the size of small peas.

2. Lightly beat an egg. Turn on the machine and immediately add the egg to the flour mixture through the feed tube, processing until the dough begins to clump together. The dough shouldn't form a mass, but it should stick together easily when pressed between the fingers. If the dough is too dry, add the optional water and process another couple of seconds.

3. Roll out the dough and shape it following the regular recipe.

TRANSPORTATION TIP

If you made this just before heading out the door, let it cool briefly and then pack it with the other hot foods.

If made ahead of time, the pie should be stored in the refrigerator and packed with the cold foods. Let it come to room temperature before eating with forks or out of hand.

You may cut it at home, leaving the pieces in place in the pie pan, or take it whole and cut and serve at meal time. Then you'll need to bring along a knife and pie server.

SIDE DISHES

DEVILED EGGS

COLE SLAW

GREEN BEANS WITH BASIL DRESSING

RED PEPPER SALAD

SAVORY BEAN SALAD

DILLED TOMATOES AND CUCUMBERS

SAUCED CARROTS, ZUCCHINI, AND RED ONIONS

ASPARAGUS IN LEMON SAUCE

RATATOUILLE

NEW POTATO SALAD

CREAM CHEESE AND OLIVE MACARONI SALAD

RICE SALAD WITH RED AND YELLOW PEPPERS

FRUIT SALAD WITH HONEY DRESSING

SWEET POTATO SALAD WITH

PINEAPPLE AND RAISINS

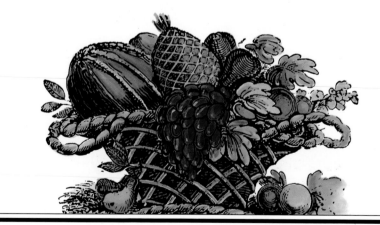

Deviled Eggs

Have you noticed that deviled eggs never go begging? Even people who normally don't eat eggs will quietly tuck away two or three halves whenever these appear on a table.

Fortunately, they're also easy to make. The most difficult part of this recipe is accurately timing the eggs so that an unappealing green ring doesn't develop around the edge of the yolk.

6 eggs
1 teaspoon vinegar (optional)
3 to 4 tablespoons good-quality mayonnaise
1 teaspoon prepared, Dijon or Durkee's mustard
Dash of curry powder
Salt and freshly ground black pepper
Small pieces of pimiento or chopped pistachios for
garnish

1. Place the eggs in a saucepan and cover by ½-inch with cold water. (Add 1 teaspoon of vinegar if cooking in an untreated aluminum pot to prevent discoloration of the pan.) Bring to a boil over high heat. Immediately reduce heat so the water barely bubbles and continue to cook, uncovered, for 10 minutes. Remove from the heat, drain, and place the eggs under cold, running water to stop the cooking. When cool enough to handle, gently tap the eggs all over to crack the shell before peeling it off.

2. Cut the tip off each end of the egg to create a flat surface for the egg to stand on. Cut each egg in half through the middle, instead of lengthwise.

3. Lift out the yolks and press through a sieve into a bowl or place all the yolks in a bowl and mash with a fork. Blend in the mayonnaise and mustard and season with curry powder, salt, and pepper.

4. Place the egg white halves in an empty egg carton and spoon a portion of the egg yolk mixture into each indentation. Garnish with diced pimiento or chopped pistachios. Transport the eggs in the closed carton. Because each egg half has a flat base on which to rest, the eggs can be set out on a plate for serving.

Makes 6 servings

TRANSPORTATION TIP

Cutting the eggs in half around the middle makes carrying them to the picnic ever so much easier. Stored in an egg carton, they are securely nestled, with no danger of tipping over.

Keep them in the carton in the refrigerator, loosely covering the filling with plastic wrap, until ready to pack. Then transfer the eggs to the cold food cooler. Just be sure the carton rests horizontally.

Should you rather not use the egg-carton method for transportation, there's no reason why the eggs and stuffing can't be carried separately to the picnic site and combined on the spot. In that case, you might want to eliminate the garnish.

Cole Slaw

During the winter I associate cole slaw with fried fish and barbecued pork sandwiches. But in the warmer months—and especially when it comes to portable meals—my horizons expand considerably, and I'll pair cole slaw with almost anything. It is, after all, a straightforward green salad, meant to marinate in its dressing for extended periods of time.

¹/₂ pound (half small head) red cabbage
¹/₂ pound (half small head) green cabbage
2 carrots

Dressing:
1 tablespoon apple cider vinegar
1 tablespoon granulated sugar
1 cup good-quality mayonnaise
Salt and freshly ground white pepper

1. Peel off the outer, limp leaves of both cabbages and remove the core. Cut each half in half again and cut long, thin shreds, using a sharp knife or food processor slicing disk. Peel the carrots and coarsely shred. To do this using the grating disc in a food processor: Cut the carrots into 2-inch lengths, stack horizontally in the feed tube, and apply heavy pressure to get thick shreds. Mix the cabbage and carrots together in a bowl.

2. To make the dressing: Place the vinegar and sugar in a small mixing bowl and stir to dissolve the sugar. Whisk in the mayonnaise until completely smooth and season with salt and pepper.

3. Pour the dressing over the grated vegetables and toss to mix thoroughly. Check the seasoning again and store, in a covered container, in the refrigerator.

Makes 6 servings

TRANSPORTATION TIP

Keep the cole slaw covered and refrigerated until you are ready to leave. Then pack it with the other cold foods.

Should you anticipate some jostling in transport, be sure that the container is tightly sealed to keep the sauce in place.

Don't forget a serving spoon.

Green Beans with Basil Dressing

Tiny, tender green beans are a spring and fall delicacy. Even if it requires spending extra time selecting the thinnest, most perfect ones from a mixed-bag assortment of sizes, go to the trouble because it's worth the effort. Not only do the younger beans taste better, they also look more attractive on the plate.

3/4 pound tiny green beans
Salt
Dressing:
 1 egg
 3 tablespoons red wine vinegar
 1 small garlic clove, peeled and flattened
 1 tablespoon chopped fresh basil or 1/2 teaspoon
  dried
 1/2 teaspoon chopped fresh tarragon or 1/4
  teaspoon dried
 1/4 teaspoon fennel seed
 Salt
 1/4 cup olive oil
 1/4 cup peanut oil

1. Cut or snap the ends off the green beans and drop into a saucepan of boiling, salted water. Cook, uncovered, 8 to 10 minutes, or until they are bright green and barely tender. Immediately remove from the heat, drain, and quickly rinse under cold, running water to stop the cooking and retain the vibrant color of the beans. Dry the beans on paper toweling and then place them in a bowl or rectangular-shaped serving dish.

2. To make the dressing: Place the egg, vinegar, garlic, basil, tarragon, fennel and salt in a blender or food processor and mix thoroughly. With the motor running, slowly add the olive oil in a thin stream. Then do the same with the peanut oil.

3. Pour a portion of the dressing over the green beans, toss, cover, and let marinate for several hours. Store any remaining dressing in a separate container and use on a simple green salad.

Makes 6 servings

TRANSPORTATION TIP

If the green beans are stored in a container with a tight-fitting lid, it's possible to occasionally turn the whole thing upside down and back to recoat the beans with dressing. It's quick and easy, and the beans don't get broken in the process. Of course the container ends up with sauce all over it, so just before serving at the picnic you might want to transfer this side dish to a clean bowl.

Take this to the picnic packed with the other cold foods. And remember to bring a serving spoon.

Red Pepper Salad

Red bell peppers are as sweet as the green ones are sharp. When roasted, that fine flavor becomes even more pronounced and pairs nicely with thin slices of fresh basil. Little else need be done to this salad; it is the well-defined tastes and fiery good looks that make this side dish special.

> *4 large red bell peppers*
> *2 tablespoons fresh basil leaves*

Dressing:
> *2 tablespoons balsamic or apple cider vinegar (see note)*
> *¼ cup good-quality olive oil*
> *Salt*

1. Heat the oven to 500° F. Put the red peppers on a baking sheet and place in the hot oven to sear for 15 minutes. When they have brown spots and the surface of the skin begins to crack and bubble, remove from the oven and place in a colander under cold, running water for a minute to stop cooking.

2. When the peppers have cooled enough to handle, peel off the skin and trim away any black spots on the peppers. Cut out the core, remove all the seeds and slice lengthwise into long, thin strips. Place in a mixing or serving bowl.

3. Stack the fresh basil leaves and cut crosswise into thin strips. Mix the basil with the red pepper.

4. To make the dressing: Place the vinegar in a small mixing bowl and gradually whisk in the olive oil. Season with salt and pour over the vegetables. Let the ingredients marinate in the refrigerator for several hours before serving.

Makes 6 servings

Note: Balsamic vinegar is available in specialty food shops.

TRANSPORTATION TIP

Store this salad in a container with a tight-fitting lid, and keep it refrigerated until ready to pack with the other cold foods.

This salad is attractive enough that you may want to transfer it to a special serving plate once you've arrived at your destination. Also bring along a serving utensil.

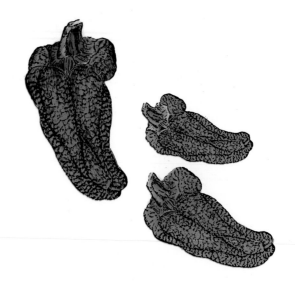

Savory Bean Salad

The traditional three-bean salad may well have been invented by a last-minute picnicker who needed a side dish in a hurry, one that could literally be pulled off the pantry shelf.

The version that appears here follows the same guidelines, only the beans and dressing have been changed around to create a pretty, delicate combination of round, oval, and elongated shapes and soft, light browns and yellow-greens. The purple-hull peas add accents of reddish-brown. The summer savory refreshes.

1 can (16 ounces) baby lima beans
1 can (15¹/₂ ounces) chick-peas (garbanzo beans)
1 can (16 ounces) cut wax beans
1 can (16 ounces) peas, preferably the fresh
*   purple-hull variety*

Dressing:
¹/₄ cup granulated sugar
¹/₃ cup white wine vinegar
1 tablespoon dried summer savory
¹/₂ cup mild-flavored olive oil
Salt and freshly ground black pepper

1. Thoroughly drain the beans and peas and rinse any that come in a sauce. Place all the vegetables in a large mixing bowl and gently toss to mix them together.

2. To make the dressing: Place the sugar, vinegar, summer savory, and salt and pepper in a blender or food processor and mix thoroughly. Gradually add the olive oil and blend thoroughly until the mixture is creamy.

3. Pour the dressing over the beans and peas. Cover and refrigerate at least 8 hours. Gently toss the vegetables every now and then to be sure all have a chance to rest in the sauce. The longer this salad stands the better it tastes.

Makes 10 to 12 servings

TRANSPORTATION TIP

Store this salad in a container with a tight-fitting lid and turn it back and forth every so often to recoat the beans with dressing. That eliminates the need to mix with a spoon and keeps the beans attractively whole. Take the salad to the picnic packed with other cold foods.

When it comes times to eat, you can serve it directly from the traveling container. Otherwise, bring along a special serving dish. In either case, don't forget the serving spoon.

Dilled Tomatoes and Cucumbers

Probably the best way to eat fresh, luscious tomatoes in the summertime is out of hand, ripe from the vine. But when straightforward begins to get boring, try this combination of tomatoes and cucumbers. Two summertime favorites—combined with dill—are united here with a luscious light tomato dressing. And if you have canned the tomato juice yourself, so much the better.

2 fresh, ripe tomatoes
2 cucumbers
Dressing:
¹/₂ cup tomato juice
¹/₄ cup olive oil
2 tablespoons white wine vinegar
2 tablespoons fresh dill or 2 teaspoons dried
1 exceptionally small garlic clove, peeled
Salt and freshly ground black pepper

1. Halve the tomatoes around the midsection and lift out the seeds with the fingers. Cut each half into 8 wedges.

2. Peel the cucumbers and cut in half lengthwise. Scoop out the seeds with a spoon and cut in ¹/₂-inch thick slices. Place the chunks of cucumber on paper towels and let drain for 10 minutes. Place the tomatoes and cucumbers in a mixing or serving bowl.

3. To make the dressing: Place all the ingredients for the dressing in a blender or food processor and mix thoroughly. Pour the dressing over the vegetables and let marinate in the refrigerator several hours.

Makes 6 servings

TRANSPORTATION TIP

Keep the tomatoes and cucumbers refrigerated in a container with a tight-fitting lid until ready to pack. At that point, transfer them to the cooler with the other cold foods.

Either serve directly from the storage container or transfer to a serving plate. For both methods you'll need to bring a large spoon.

Sauced Carrots, Zucchini, and Red Onions

Carrot sticks are, no doubt, the all-time easiest vegetable to pack up and carry out. Look at how long they've been a staple of the brown bag lunch.

You may, however, modernize this classic by adding traveling companions and lightly dressing the resulting blend with a vinaigrette. The carrots retain all their crunchy texture while the zucchini and onions soften just enough not to taste raw.

2 medium carrots
2 medium zucchini
^{1}/2 medium purple onion, cut through the root end

Dressing:

3 tablespoons white wine vinegar
1 teaspoon granulated sugar
2 teaspoons fresh marjoram leaves or ^{1}/2 teaspoon dried
Salt and freshly ground black pepper
^{1}/3 cup mild-flavored olive oil

1. Peel and trim the carrots and cut into 1^1/2-inch lengths. Stand the carrots on end and cut into ^{1}/4-inch slices. Stack several slices and cut into ^{1}/4-inch matchsticks.

2. Do not peel the zucchini, but trim the ends and cut into 1^1/2-inch lengths also. Cut, like the carrots, into matchstick lengths.

3. Lay the onion on its cut side and slice in half again, lengthwise, going through the root end. Now slice the two sections crosswise into ^{1}/4-inch half strips. Place the carrots, zucchini, and onion in a mixing or serving bowl and toss to combine the ingredients.

4. To make the dressing: Place the vinegar, sugar, marjoram, and salt and pepper in a blender or food processor. With the motor running, slowly add the olive oil until the mixture is well blended. Pour the dressing over the vegetables and let marinate in the refrigerator several hours.

Makes 6 servings

TRANSPORTATION TIP

This side dish travels best in a container with a tight-fitting lid so that nothing can spill. Keep it refrigerated until ready to pack it with other cold foods.

It can be served directly from the storage container or it can be transferred to another dish you've brought along. A slotted spoon works best for serving.

Asparagus in Lemon Sauce

Some people insist that thick stalks of asparagus are more flavorful, but I happen to like the pencil-thin ones myself. It also feels like I'm getting more per pound when I buy the slender ones, and that visual trick pays off in the early spring when the price of asparagus is still sky high.

For hot asparagus, nothing beats lemon butter—or, of course, hollandaise. When served cold, an easy, ersatz version of that sauce is just as exquisite.

> *1 pound pencil-thin asparagus, trimmed to*
> *6-inch lengths*
> *Salt*

Sauce:
> *²/₃ cup good-quality mayonnaise*
> *1 teaspoon prepared mustard*
> *1¹/₂ tablespoons fresh lemon juice*
> *Salt*

1. Drop the asparagus in boiling, salted water and cook 5 minutes, or until bright green and barely tender. Immediately drain and quickly rinse under cold, running water to stop the cooking and retain the vibrant color. Lay the asparagus on paper toweling to dry. Then place in a serving dish, all stalks heading in the same direction.

2. To make the dressing: Whisk the mayonnaise and mustard together in a small mixing bowl. Gradually stir in the lemon juice and season with salt. Put this dressing in a separate dish and place a dollop of the sauce on the asparagus as it is served.

Makes 6 servings

TRANSPORTATION TIP

Refrigerate the asparagus and the sauce separately. The sauce should be tightly sealed—a small jar works fine—but the asparagus needs only to be wrapped in aluminum foil. When ready to leave for your outing, pack both items with other cold foods.

Bring along asparagus tongs, if you have them. Otherwise an extra fork will do. The sauce will need a spoon.

Ratatouille

This chunky vegetable stew is normally served hot, but it tastes equally good warm and some people even like it cold. While it looks fairly dark and sober, the red bell peppers and the dark skin on the eggplant add visual interest, while the garlic, anchovies, and hot pepper-flavored olive oil give it considerable zing. Should you like yours really spicy, simply leave some of the hot peppers in place—giving other diners fair warning, of course.

⅓ cup olive oil

1 small hot red pepper, seeded and chopped

3 large garlic cloves, peeled and flattened

2 small eggplants (each 1 pound), cut into ½-inch cubes

2 medium red bell peppers, seeded and diced

2 cans (each 14½ ounces) plum tomatoes with tomato juice reserved, or 2 cups fresh, ripe plum tomatoes, coarsely chopped

½ cup tomato juice (optional, see step 3)

4 medium scallions, trimmed to 6-inch lengths and chopped

5 anchovy fillets, minced

⅓ cup, loosely packed, chopped fresh parsley

2 tablespoons fresh marjoram leaves or 1 teaspoon dried

Salt (optional)

1. Heat the olive oil in a large frying pan over medium heat and add the hot pepper and garlic. Cook 5 to 7 minutes until the peppers and garlic begin to brown, then lift them out of the oil and discard.

2. Turn the heat to medium-low and add the eggplants and red bell peppers to the seasoned oil. Cook the vegetables 5 to 7 minutes until they begin to soften.

3. If using canned tomatoes, drain off the tomato juice and reserve. Coarsely chop the tomatoes and add to the mixture in the frying pan along with ½ cup of the reserved juice. (Save any remaining juice from the canned tomatoes for another use.) If using fresh tomatoes, add the 2 cups along with ½ cup tomato juice. Bring this mixture to a boil, lower the heat, and let the sauce reduce for 3 or 4 minutes.

4. Add the scallions and anchovies and continue cooking about 5 minutes before seasoning with the parsley and marjoram. Simmer only briefly at this point. Almost all of the moisture should have evaporated by now and the vegetables should be tender but not mushy. Taste and add salt, or another anchovy, if desired.

Makes 6 servings

TRANSPORTATION TIP

Store the ratatouille in a covered dish in the refrigerator, then transfer it to the cooler alongside other cold foods. This is a thick mixture, so don't worry if it gets jostled around slightly. There is little liquid to spill.

Either serve as is or transfer it to a fancier dish when you reach your destination. Remember to bring a serving spoon.

New Potato Salad

New potatoes, with their jackets on, add a rustic air to this ever-popular summer side dish. The rest of the recipe, however, follows long-standing principles: a hint of celery, lots of hard-cooked eggs and parsley, and mayonnaise thinned with sour cream. The combination produces a smooth flavor and sunny appearance.

2 pounds new potatoes (10 small ones,
*   approximately 1 1/2 inches in diameter)*
Salt
4 eggs
1 teaspoon vinegar (optional)
1 celery rib, finely diced (2 tablespoons)
1/4 cup, loosely packed, finely chopped fresh
*   parsley*
1/2 cup good-quality mayonnaise
1/4 cup sour cream
1 teaspoon sweet mustard
Freshly ground black pepper

1. Place the unpeeled potatoes in a large saucepan and cover by 1 inch with cold water. Add 1/2 teaspoon salt and bring to a boil. Lower the heat and cook at a gentle boil 15 to 20 minutes, or until the tip of a knife slips easily into a potato. Drain and cool before cutting into quarters or eighths.

2. Place the eggs in a saucepan and cover by 1/2 inch with cold water. (Add 1 teaspoon of vinegar if cooking in an untreated aluminum pot to prevent discoloration of the pan.) Bring to a boil and then immediately reduce the heat so the water barely bubbles. Continue to cook, uncovered, for 10 minutes. Remove from heat, drain, and place the eggs under cold, running water to stop the cooking. When cool enough to handle, gently tap the egg all over to crack the shell before peeling it off. Cut the eggs into small chunks.

3. Place the potatoes, eggs, celery, shallots, and parsley in a mixing bowl and toss gently to mix everything together.

4. In a separate mixing bowl, blend together the mayonnaise, sour cream, and sweet mustard. Pour this mixture over the potatoes and toss again to blend the flavors and coat the vegetables. Taste and season with salt and pepper.

Makes 6 servings

TRANSPORTATION TIP

Keep the potato salad refrigerated in a covered dish until you are ready to go. At that point, carry it along with other cold foods.

It can easily be served from its container; simply bring along a large spoon.

Cream Cheese and Olive Macaroni Salad

Obviously, it was the memory of a cream cheese and olive sandwich that inspired this side dish. Only instead of sandwiching this silky smooth, sharp-tasting mixture between slices of bread, it's combined here with macaroni. The only difficulty was deciding whether to use the ripe black or the pimiento-stuffed green olives, and I finally opted for both. If you're looking for a comfort food, this is it.

1 1/2 cups small elbow macaroni
1 teaspoon vegetable oil
1 3/4 cups pitted black olives cut in wedges
1/2 cup pimiento-stuffed green olives cut in wedges
3/4 cup drained garbanzo beans
3 tablespoons finely chopped fresh parsley
8 ounces cream cheese, softened
1/2 cup good-quality mayonnaise
3 tablespoons milk
Salt and freshly ground black pepper
2 cherry tomatoes, quartered, for garnish

1. Bring a large quantity of salted water to a boil and cook the macaroni according to the directions on the package. As soon as the pasta is al dente, drain and toss with the oil.

2. Place the macaroni in a large mixing bowl and add the black and green olives, the garbanzo beans, and the parsley. Gently toss together so everything is mixed.

3. Put the cream cheese in another mixing bowl and smear it around the bowl until it is smooth. Add the mayonnaise and milk and blend thoroughly once again. Season with salt and pepper and pour over the macaroni mixture. Stir and toss carefully to blend all the ingredients and coat them with the cream cheese. Transfer to a serving dish and garnish with cherry tomatoes. The salad may be covered and refrigerated, but be sure it is warm before serving.

Makes 6 servings

TRANSPORTATION TIP

This salad will need to be refrigerated if you make it ahead of time; however, it is best when brought back to room temperature before serving. So if the picnic site is close by, don't bother packing it with the cold foods. By the time you arrive it will be perfect for eating. On the longer journey, keep it with the cold foods, but bring it out of storage in time for it to loosen up.

It can travel, covered up with aluminum foil or plastic wrap, in its serving dish.

Rice Salad with Red and Yellow Peppers

The red and yellow peppers in this celebratory side dish look like colorful confetti. Their intriguing sweet and piquant flavor combines well with the nutty basmati rice and buttery pine nuts.

2 cups water
½ teaspoon salt
1 cup basmati-type or long-grain rice (see note)
2 tablespoons peanut oil
½ cup pine nuts
2 tablespoons unsalted butter
1 medium red bell pepper, seeded and diced
1 medium yellow bell pepper, seeded and diced
1 tablespoon apple cider vinegar

1. Bring the water to a boil in a medium saucepan and add the salt and rice. Stir and bring the water back to a boil. Immediately reduce the heat to low and leave uncovered, with the water barely bubbling until it has cooked down to the level of the rice. Now cover and simmer 5 minutes. Remove from the heat, leaving the lid in place, and let rest 5 to 10 minutes before using.

2. Place the oil in a frying pan over medium-high heat, and when hot add the pine nuts. Let them bubble and cook a minute or two until lightly golden brown. Lift the pine nuts out of the oil with a slotted spoon and set aside.

3. Add the butter to the oil remaining in the frying pan and stir in the diced red and yellow peppers. Reduce the heat to medium and gently sauté the vegetables 5 or 6 minutes until tender. Finally, add the vinegar and cook 2 or 3 minutes, until it has evaporated.

4. Gently stir the cooked rice into the vegetable mixture and then transfer everything to a serving dish. Cover and store in the refrigerator.

Makes 6 servings

Note: Available at specialty food shops.

TRANSPORTATION TIP

Keep the rice salad cold until ready to pack up. It can travel with the other cold foods, but on a short excursion it will do fine without being chilled. Just be sure it's covered, and remember a spoon to dish it up.

Fruit Salad with Honey Dressing

Almost any mixture of fruits would go well here, but the flavors of papaya, grapes, kiwi, and honeydew combine especially well with the taste of the malted honey dressing.

The blend of malted milk and honey, apricot nectar and apple cider vinegar may sound strange, but it ends up tasting heavenly, enhanced by its beautiful soft, peachy color.

1 large papaya

1 medium honeydew melon

2 kiwis

3 cups seedless green grapes

Malted Honey Dressing:

³/4 cup apricot nectar

3 tablespoons instant, natural-flavored malted milk

3 tablespoons raw honey

1¹/2 teaspoons apple cider vinegar

1. Peel and seed the papaya. Slice crosswise into short, thin strips.

2. Cut the melon in half, remove the seeds and membrane, and scoop out melon balls.

3. Peel the kiwis and cut crosswise into thin rounds. Stack the slices and cut in half.

4. Cut the grapes in half. Combine all the fruits in a large mixing bowl.

5. To make the dressing: Place all the ingredients in a blender or food processor and mix until thoroughly smooth and creamy. Pour over the fruit, cover, and refrigerate for several hours. Stir the mixture occasionally so all the fruit blends with the sauce.

Makes 6 servings

TRANSPORTATION TIP

Store the fruit salad in a container with a tight-fitting lid, occasionally turning it upside down and moving it back and forth to effortlessly mix the ingredients. When leaving for the picnic, transfer the container to the cooler with other cold foods.

It may be served from this dish or another more stylish one you've brought along, depending on your mood. Dish it up using a tablespoon.

Sweet Potato Salad with Pineapple and Raisins

When you've had enough of regular potato salad, try this one for a different sensation. The bright pineapple, together with the deep orange potatoes and the light and dark raisins, combine to create golden good looks and even better taste. To carry the effect further, juice from the pineapple gets blended into the dressing.

1 ½ pounds sweet potatoes (4 small ones, about 3 inches long)
½ teaspoon salt
1 can (8 ounces) sliced pineapple, drained and juice reserved
¼ cup golden raisins
¼ cup dark seedless raisins

Dressing:
1 egg yolk
½ cup light brown sugar
¼ cup pineapple juice, reserved from the juice of the sliced pineapple
2 tablespoons apple cider vinegar
½ cup vegetable oil

1. Place the sweet potatoes in a large saucepan and cover by 1 inch with cold water. Add ½ teaspoon salt and bring to a boil. Lower the heat and gently cook about 15 minutes, or just until the tip of a paring knife slips easily into a potato. Drain and briefly place under cold, running water to stop the cooking. Cool completely, peel off the skin, and cut into slices ⅜-inch thick. Place the slices in a large, shallow baking pan.

2. Cut the drained pineapple into small wedges and add to the potato slices along with the golden and dark raisins.

3. To make the dressing: Place the egg yolk, brown sugar, pineapple juice, and vinegar in a blender or food processor. Mix completely so that the sugar is almost dissolved. Then, with the motor running, slowly add the oil in a thin stream.

4. Pour the dressing over the potato mixture, cover, and refrigerate. Gently stir the potatoes occasionally to make sure the dressing coats the salad completely. Transfer to a dish before serving.

Makes 6 servings

TRANSPORTATION TIP

While this salad is resting in the refrigerator, keep it in a broad, shallow dish so all the potatoes come in contact with the dressing. For packing, however, it should be transferred to a covered container that can double as a serving dish. It gets packed with other cold foods.

Take along a large spoon for serving.

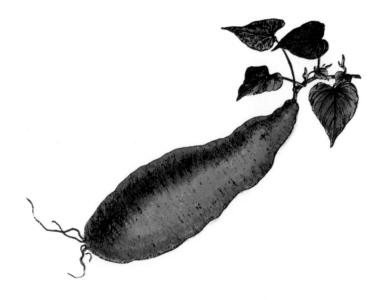

BREADS

POCKETBOOK ROLLS
HERB-CHEESE PULLMAN SANDWICH LOAF
CINNAMON-NUT SANDWICH LOAF
CORNMEAL MUFFINS
OATMEAL SPICE MUFFINS
WHOLE-WHEAT ROLLS WITH
SUNFLOWER KERNELS
CORNMEAL SODA CRACKERS
PLAIN SODA CRACKERS

Pocketbook Rolls

Sometimes going under the name Parker House rolls, these soft-as-a-cloud bits of bread have been folded in half before baking. This means they can be opened up once they're cooked—just like a pocketbook—so that something can be put inside. Plain butter fits well in these culinary purses, but you can stuff them with small pieces of meat and turn them into miniature sandwiches.

1 cup milk
¼ cup vegetable shortening
2 tablespoons granulated sugar
1¼ teaspoons salt
1 package fast-acting yeast
2 eggs
3 to 3¼ cups flour
4 tablespoons unsalted butter, melted

1. Place the milk, shortening, sugar and salt in a saucepan over low heat and stir until the ingredients are completely dissolved. Remove from the heat when the temperature reaches 115° F.

2. Put 2 cups of the flour into a food processor fitted with the plastic blade and add the fast-acting yeast, eggs, and milk mixture. Process a full 5 minutes until the batter has thickened slightly and is somewhat elastic. Stop occasionally to stir down the sides of the bowl.

3. Add another 1 cup flour and process 1 minute. The dough will be loose and stretchy and will not have formed a mass. Add an additional ¼ cup of flour if necessary, but not so much that a clump of dough forms.

4. Scrape the dough into a clean, lightly greased bowl. Cover with plastic wrap and set in a warm spot (80 to 85° F.) to proof about 45 minutes, or until the dough has expanded to double its original size.

5. Brush a little of the melted butter over a 15½ x 10½ x 1-inch jelly-roll pan. Keep the remaining butter warm.

6. Stir down the dough to break the big air pockets, then scrape out onto a heavily floured, smooth work surface. Flour the top of the dough and pat or gently roll until it is ⅜ inch thick.

7. Dip a 2¾-inch biscuit cutter in flour and press out 24 rounds of dough. Jiggle the cutter back and forth to separate each round from the whole piece.

8. Gently pick up a round of dough with your fingers and barely dip half of one side in the melted butter. Place it on the greased pan with the buttered portion up, fold the round in half so the butter is in the middle, and lightly flatten the half-moon shape. Space the rolls about ½ inch apart. There should be room for three rolls going one way and eight the other.

9. Cover the rolls on the pan with a tea towel and place in a warm spot for about 30 minutes, or until the rolls have doubled in bulk. Meanwhile, heat the oven to 425°F.

10. Bake 8 to 10 minutes or until golden brown on top. Remove the sheet from the oven and immediately brush the rolls with the remaining butter. If not eating immediately, tightly cover the cooled rolls with plastic wrap or store in plastic bags.

Makes 24 small rolls

TRANSPORTATION TIP

If the rolls have been made within hours of packing, simply cover them with foil or plastic wrap as they rest in the baking pan and serve them from it.

If you've made them further in advance, they'll stay fresh best when stored in sealed plastic bags. They may also be frozen, if tightly wrapped in plastic or foil.

Herb-Cheese Pullman Sandwich Loaf

It's unclear how the pullman loaf pan, with its lid that slides in place to encase the rising dough, got its name. Perhaps someone thought it resembled the pullman suitcase, with its lid that snaps down to entrap the items in one of the halves. Or the name could go back to the pullman kitchen, which boasted a double door that swung open to reveal the kitchen work space and shut to block out the clutter. It's even possible that the pan was named after the pullman railway car, where passengers slept in neatly and compactly enclosed compartments.

No matter how you look at it, however, this pan makes bread baking a tidy affair, and it's worth a trip to a specialty shop to invest in one. By using this loaf pan, the top of the bread comes out as flat as the bottom, with all four sides almost equal in measurement. As a side benefit, the containing process ensures a fine-textured bread, which, in this case, is visually enhanced by a swirl of seasoning rolled into the loaf while it is shaped.

Dough:
> 6 cups unbleached all-purpose flour
> 1/2 cup unsalted butter, cut into pieces and
>   softened
> 2 packages fast-acting yeast
> 1 tablespoon granulated sugar
> 1 tablespoon salt
> 1 1/2 cups hot water (115° F.)
> 2 tablespoons unsalted butter, melted

Filling:
> 1/2 cup finely and freshly grated Parmesan cheese
> 1 teaspoon Hungarian paprika
> 1 teaspoon dried marjoram
> 1/2 teaspoon dried basil

1. To make the dough: Place the flour and butter in a large mixing bowl and rub the mixture between the fingers until the butter is in fine pieces and almost absorbed in the flour.

2. Add the yeast, sugar, and salt. Mix thoroughly and then add the hot water. Stir and eventually work with the hands until a dough forms and cleans the bowl.

3. Turn the dough out onto a clean work surface and knead 8 to 10 minutes or until smooth and shiny. Because this dough is buttery, it should easily pull off the counter even though it looks like it is sticking. The longer it is kneaded, the easier it is to work. Lightly flour the hands, if necessary, for easier handling.

4. Place the dough in an ungreased large mixing bowl and cover with plastic wrap. Set the bowl in a warm spot (80 to 85° F.) to proof about 45 minutes.

5. Mix the filling while waiting for the dough to rise: Place the Parmesan cheese, paprika, marjoram and basil in a small mixing bowl and stir to blend. Also butter the inside of a 13 x 4 x 4-inch pullman loaf pan and the bottom of the lid. Heat the oven to 400° F.

6. When the dough has expanded to double its original size, punch it down and knead it lightly for 30 seconds before shaping into a flattened round. Lightly flour both sides of the dough before rolling out into a 14 x 14-inch square.

7. Brush the top side of the dough with butter and sprinkle the cheese-herb mixture over the entire surface. Roll up tightly, pull the top layer of dough down over the ends to enclose them, and place the loaf, seam side down, in the pullman loaf pan.

8. Set in a warm spot and let rise until the dough almost comes to the top of the loaf pan. (There must be some breathing space in order to slip on the lid. The dough will rise further in the first minutes of baking.) Bake 50 to 60 minutes. When the lid is removed the crust should be golden brown on all sides and the loaf should sound hollow when tapped. Turn out onto a wire rack to cool completely before storing or slicing.

Makes 1 long loaf

VARIATION

Cinnamon-Nut Sandwich Loaf

Make the loaf as directed above, substituting the following filling, made by mixing together:

¹/₄ cup granulated sugar
¹/₄ cup very finely chopped pecans
1 teaspoon ground cinnamon

TRANSPORTATION TIP

Pullman loaf bread stores well wrapped in plastic. It can be refrigerated for a couple of days or frozen for a month.

Keeping the loaf whole helps it stay moist, so don't cut it until sandwich-making time. If this means at the picnic site, be sure to bring along a serrated bread knife for easy slicing.

This bread doesn't need to travel in a cooler unless you've already made the sandwiches. In that case, they should be stored with other cold foods.

Cornmeal Muffins

One southern wag has claimed that muffins only came into existence because northerners couldn't make biscuits. I prefer to think they were invented by a cook who simply wanted to make a quick bread in even more of a hurry. So instead of making a big loaf, the baker divided the batter into individual servings before baking to save time.

The sour cream used in this recipe gives the muffin its tender, moist crumb. One, incidentally, that holds up well a day after baking.

> *1 egg*
> *1 cup sour cream*
> *3 tablespoons granulated sugar*
> *½ cup stoneground yellow cornmeal*
> *½ cup unbleached all-purpose flour*
> *1 teaspoon baking powder*
> *½ teaspoon baking soda*
> *½ teaspoon salt*

1. Thoroughly grease a 6-cup, standard-size muffin tin, coating both the indentations and the top of the pan. Heat the oven to 400° F.

2. Place the egg, sour cream, and sugar in a mixing bowl and beat with a whisk until smooth and creamy.

3. Stir together or sift the cornmeal, flour, baking powder, baking soda and salt to mix thoroughly. Then add the dry ingredients to the egg–sour cream mixture. Stir just until the dry ingredients are completely moistened.

4. Spoon the batter into the muffin cups, filling to the top. Place in the oven and bake 15 to 18 minutes, or until nicely browned. Let rest in the pan 2 or 3 minutes before turning out on a wire rack to cool.

Makes 6 large muffins

VARIATION

Oatmeal Spice Muffins

Follow the recipe above, eliminating the ½ cup cornmeal, and adding in its place:

> *½ cup oatmeal*
> *⅓ cup chopped pecans*
> *¼ cup golden raisins*
> *½ teaspoon ground cinnamon*
> *¼ teaspoon freshly grated nutmeg*

Makes 6 very large muffins.

TRANSPORTATION TIP

These muffins can be made a day in advance, cooled, and then wrapped in plastic or put in a plastic container with a tight-fitting lid for storage and transportation at room temperature. They retain their moisture remarkably well and can be frozen if you want to make them several days in advance, but making muffins is so simple, you may never need to do that.

To warm the muffins, wrap them in aluminum foil and place in an oven heated to 350° F. for 7 or 8 minutes. Take these to the picnic packed with other hot foods.

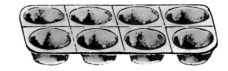

Whole-Wheat Rolls with Sunflower Kernels

Fast-acting yeast has revolutionized bread baking. What used to be an almost all-day affair has been pared down to a two-hour project. Everything happens so quick now you barely have a chance to clean up the kitchen before the bread's out of the oven. A little of the slowly developed, yeasty quality of the loaf may be lost in the process, but the wonderful home-baked quality remains.

2 cups bread flour
1 1/2 to 1 3/4 cups whole-wheat flour
2 tablespoons unsalted sunflower kernels
2 teaspoons salt
2 packages fast-acting yeast
2 tablespoons vegetable oil
1 1/4 cups hot water (115° F.)

1. Place the bread flour and 1 1/2 cups of whole-wheat flour in a large mixing bowl and stir in the sunflower kernels, salt, and fast-acting yeast. Then add the vegetable oil and hot water. Stir and eventually work with the hands until a dough forms and cleans the bowl.

2. Turn the dough out onto a lightly floured work surface and knead about 10 minutes, or until it is smooth and elastic. Keep the hands dusted with flour if the dough seems damp. Add as little extra flour to the dough as possible.

3. Place the kneaded dough in a lightly greased, large mixing bowl. Cover the bowl with plastic wrap and set in a warm spot (80 to 85° F.) to proof about 45 minutes, or until the dough has expanded to double its original size.

4. Punch down the dough and knead lightly about 10 seconds. Shape the dough into two flattened rounds. Cut both into 8 equal-sized wedges. Shape each piece into a ball, rolling the dough on a smooth work surface in a tight circle under the light pressure of the cupped palm of the hand.

5. Place on baking sheets lined with parchment paper and spray with a fine mist of water. Let the rolls proof, uncovered, 30 to 45 minutes or until they have almost tripled in size. Meanwhile heat the oven to 400° F.

6. Mist the rolls again just before slipping them into the hot oven and bake 20 minutes or until lightly browned all over.

Makes 16 rolls

TRANSPORTATION TIP

If these rolls are eaten the same day they're baked, store them in a paper bag or wrapped in aluminum foil so the rolls have a chance to breathe and the crust stays crispy.

If the rolls are made a day ahead of time, they should be packed in plastic bags and stored at room temperature so they retain more of their internal moisture. This does, however, make the crust softer. If the rolls are made more than a day in advance, they should be frozen. Thaw them at least partially before packing them up with the other loose supplies.

If the picnic is on a deck or in a backyard, you will be able to reheat the rolls and serve them warm. Place the unwrapped rolls on a baking sheet and lightly mist them with water just before placing in an oven heated to 400° F. They will take only 3 or 4 minutes to heat and once again have a crispy crust.

Cornmeal Soda Crackers

Beaten biscuits, a hefty version of our modern-day cracker, originally were whacked or, literally, beaten by hand. Then someone developed a ringer attachment (much like the one on old-fashioned washing machines) to do the work instead. It must have been a wonder of modern science at the time.

Unfortunately, few modern kitchens possess one of these machines, so beaten biscuits have now been pretty much eliminated from the household culinary repertoire. But hand-crank pasta makers (in effect, small-scale versions of the biscuit machine) lurk in thousands of American cupboards, making it possible to crank out the thinner cousin of the beaten biscuit, the cracker.

The cornmeal crackers are particularly fine, but you may also make plain crackers without the cornmeal—with or without salt.

>   *2 cups self-rising flour*
>   *1/2 cup yellow cornmeal*
>   *1/4 cup shortening*
>   *3/4 teaspoon salt*
>   *1 teaspoon fast-acting yeast*
>   *1/2 cup ice-cold water*
>   *Coarse kosher salt*

1. Place the self-rising flour, cornmeal, shortening, salt, and fast-acting yeast in the bowl of a food processor fitted with the steel blade. Turn the machine on and off quickly, pulsing twelve or fourteen times until no pieces of shortening remain.

2. With the motor running, slowly pour the water into the flour. When 2 or 3 tablespoons of water are left, go even slower so the mixture has a chance to form into a ball with the least amount of water. Stop as soon as a clump of dough forms. It will feel warm and soft.

3. Remove the dough from the processor and divide into two equal pieces. Knead each one into a smooth ball and wrap in wax paper. Let the dough rest 15 minutes.

4. Heat the oven to 350° F. Line baking sheets with parchment paper.

5. Flatten one of the balls of dough to about a 1/4-inch thickness and lightly flour both sides. Crank it through the rollers of a pasta machine on the widest setting. Extend the dough and fold in thirds. Again press flat, dust with flour on both sides and roll through the widest setting, starting with one of the open ends. Continue this folding, flattening, and flouring process a total of ten to twelve times. If necessary, as the dough shrinks in this kneading process, it may only have to be folded in half to fit the full width of the rollers.

6. When the dough is smooth and elastic, begin rolling it into thinner and thinner sheets by passing the lightly floured dough through narrower and narrower roller settings. On a 6-setting machine the dough should be passed through settings 1 through 4.

7. Lay the long, thin strip of dough out on a clean work surface. Use a pastry cutter 2 to 2 1/2 inches wide to stamp out circles of dough. Prick each circle of dough three or four times with a table fork. Lift the rounds off the counter and place close together on the parchment-lined baking sheets. Sprinkle with coarse salt and bake in the heated oven for 12 to 14 minutes, or just until the rounds are beginning to turn color. The coloring happens quickly, so watch carefully. Cool on a rack and store in an airtight tin.

8. Repeat the process with the remaining piece of dough.

Makes 4 dozen crackers

Plain Soda Crackers

Eliminate the cornmeal, reduce the salt to ¼ teaspoon, and add a little less water. Other than that, proceed as above. This dough will be more elastic.

TRANSPORTATION TIP

Keep the crackers in a tightly covered metal tin at room temperature so they stay crisp. Alternatively, they may be securely wrapped in aluminum foil, but do not put them in anything plastic because they will become soggy.

The tin also travels easily to a picnic site and should not be packed in a cooler. Simply carry it with the utensils.

Should you want to make presentation special, bring along a handsome serving dish or wicker basket to hold the crackers.

DESSERTS

CHEWY MOLASSES SUGAR COOKIES
SUGAR COOKIES
CHOCOLATE RASPBERRY BARS WITH WALNUTS
TOFFEE BARS
CHOCOLATE MALTED CAKE
PEANUT BUTTER AND BANANA CAKE
ROLLED LIME CURD CAKE WITH
RASPBERRY SAUCE
STRAWBERRY SAUCE
PEACH AND CREAM CHEESE TART
APPLE TART

Chewy Molasses Sugar Cookies

Sugar cookies are probably the basic little black dress of the dessert world. Because of their delicate, mild flavor they go with just about anything. Dress them up with a little icing decoration, or dress them down with the addition of molasses, ginger, and allspice.

I prefer the spunk of molasses. No apologies here for hearty, full-bodied flavor. I happen to like mine chewy, so I bake these for a fairly brief time. Should you prefer yours crisp, cook them just a little longer. They store very well in a tightly closed tin.

¹/₂ cup shortening
³/₄ cup light brown sugar
1 egg
¹/₂ cup unsulfured molasses
2 cups all-purpose flour
1 teaspoon ground allspice
1 teaspoon ground ginger
¹/₄ teaspoon baking soda
¹/₄ teaspoon salt
¹/₃ cup granulated sugar

1. Beat the shortening and sugar together in a mixing bowl until creamy and fluffy. Add the egg and continue beating until the mixture becomes thick and silky. Now stir in the molasses.

2. Stir together or sift the flour, allspice, ginger, baking soda and salt to blend the ingredients thoroughly. Then add the dry mixture to the molasses mixture and stir until moistened. Cover the dough with wax paper and chill 1 hour.

3. Lightly grease 2 or 3 baking sheets. Place the granulated sugar in a cake pan. Set both aside. Heat the oven to 350° F.

4. Roll tablespoons of dough into 1- to 1¹/₄-inch balls. Place several of these at a time in the granulated sugar and swirl around to coat them evenly with sugar.

5. Place the rounds of dough two inches apart on the baking sheet. Dip the base of a drinking glass in the sugar and use it to flatten each cookie to a 3/16-inch thickness and 2¹/₂ inches in diameter.

6. Bake for 7 or 8 minutes. The cookies will just be set. Cool 3 or 4 minutes before removing from the baking sheet to a wire rack. When cool, store them in a tightly closed tin.

Makes 4 dozen cookies.

VARIATION

Sugar Cookies

1. Substitute unsalted butter for the shortening. Substitute granulated sugar for the brown sugar. Eliminate the molasses, allspice, and ginger. All other ingredients are the same.

2. Procedure is as follows: Cream the butter and sugar, beat in the egg, stir in the flour, baking soda and salt. Now shape the dough into a cylinder 12 inches long on wax paper. Sprinkle the rope of dough all over with granulated sugar. Refrigerate 1 to 1¹/₂ hours. Slice ¹/₄ inch thick and place on a lightly greased baking sheet. Sprinkle sugar over the tops of the cookies and bake in an oven heated to 350° F. for 7 or 8 minutes. They will be set but barely have any color on the bottom. Cool 3 or 4 minutes before removing from the pan.

TRANSPORTATION TIP

Molasses sugar cookies store and travel best at room temperature in a metal tin with a tight-fitting lid. As an alternative, they may be wrapped in aluminum foil, but avoid anything plastic so they do not become soggy.

Chocolate Raspberry Bars with Walnuts

Walnuts on top of raspberry jam on top of chocolate—a layering of dark, intense, and substantial flavors that my taste buds find both sophisticated and soul-satisfying. Cut these rich bars into fairly small portions. They should be savored—like a fine cognac—not gulped down.

> *¹/₂ cup unsalted butter, softened*
> *³/₄ cup granulated sugar*
> *1 egg, separated*
> *¹/₂ teaspoon vanilla extract*
> *³/₄ cup all-purpose flour*
> *¹/₄ cup unsweetened cocoa powder*
> *¹/₈ teaspoon salt*
> *¹/₄ cup seedless red raspberry jam*
> *¹/₄ cup chopped walnuts*
> *1 to 2 tablespoons granulated sugar, as garnish*

1. Cream the butter and ³/₄ cup sugar together in a mixing bowl until light and fluffy. Add the egg yolk and vanilla, beating until thick and silky.

2. Stir together or sift the flour, cocoa, and salt to mix thoroughly. Add this to the butter-sugar mixture and stir just until moistened.

3. Spread the dough in an ungreased 8 X 8-inch baking pan and put in the freezer to chill for 10 minutes.

4. Heat the oven to 325° F.

5. Stir the raspberry jam to make it smooth and loose. Spread it over the chilled dough and return to the freezer for 5 minutes.

6. Beat the egg white until frothy and brush about half of it over the cold raspberry jam, discarding any remainder. Scatter the walnuts on top and lightly press into place.

7. Bake in the hot oven for 35 minutes, or just until the edges begin to pull away from the sides of the pan. Remove from the oven and immediately sprinkle with the 1 to 2 tablespoons sugar. Cool in the pan before cutting into serving pieces.

Makes 16 small squares

TRANSPORTATION TIP

The chocolate raspberry bars can travel to the picnic in their baking pan, covered with aluminum foil. They don't need to be placed in a cooler.

You might want to bring along a plate to serve them on, however. And don't forget a table knife or small spatula to help lift them out.

Toffee Bars

Buttery and rich—just like toffee should be—these bars bake up thin and chewy with lots of pecans sprinkled on top to add texture and a good, nutty taste. Fortunately, this almost-like-candy confection takes very little time to prepare. So whip up a batch anytime you feel like treating yourself.

1 cup unsalted butter, softened
½ cup granulated sugar
½ cup light brown sugar
1 egg, separated
1 teaspoon vanilla extract
1½ cups all-purpose flour
¼ teaspoon salt
2 teaspoons granulated sugar
1 cup chopped pecans

1. Heat the oven to 350° F.

2. Place the butter and sugars in a large mixing bowl and beat until smooth and fluffy. Add the egg yolk and vanilla extract and continue beating until the mixture has thickened and become silky.

3. Add the flour and salt and stir just until well blended.

4. Spread the dough into an ungreased 15½ x 10½ x 1-inch jelly-roll pan. Smooth out the top.

5. Beat the egg white until foamy. Add the 2 teaspoons granulated sugar and beat until the egg white holds some shape. Brush about half of this mixture over the surface of the dough, discarding any remainder. Sprinkle the nuts over the top.

6. Bake 20 to 25 minutes, or until the top is golden brown and still a little soft. Cool 10 to 15 minutes, or until completely set, then cut into squares or diamonds and remove from the pan.

Makes about 35 toffee bars

TRANSPORTATION TIP

Covered with aluminum foil, the toffee bars can go to a picnic in their baking pan. Or if that size seems unwieldy, lift the bars out and wrap in two or three separate packages using foil.

Take along an extra serving plate for a more elegant presentation at the picnic.

Chocolate Malted Cake

As surprising as it may seem, chocolate cakes aren't everyone's favorite. One food expert claims that at least 3 percent of the population would prefer to eat angel food or even golden chiffon. I say, let them. Diversity is what made this country great. But if you're interested in pleasing the rest of the masses, this chocolate dessert will—as the saying goes—knock their socks off.

1/2 cup unsalted butter, softened

1 1/4 cups granulated sugar

2 eggs

1 cup cake flour

1/2 cup unsweetened cocoa powder

3 tablespoons instant natural-flavored malted milk powder

1/2 teaspoon baking soda

1/2 teaspoon baking powder

1/4 teaspoon salt

3/4 cup buttermilk

Chocolate Icing:

2 ounces semisweet chocolate

2 tablespoons heavy whipping cream

1 tablespoon unsalted butter, softened

1. To make the cake: Butter a 9-inch springform pan. Line the bottom with a circle of wax paper and lightly butter that also.

2. Place the butter and sugar in a mixing bowl and beat until the mixture is smooth and fluffy. Then beat in the eggs one at a time, making sure the mixture thickens and becomes silky before adding another egg.

3. Stir together or sift the flour, cocoa, malted milk, baking soda, baking powder, and salt to mix thoroughly. Add half of this to the butter-sugar mixture and stir just enough to blend. Add all the buttermilk and stir until smooth, then blend in the remaining dry ingredients.

4. Pour this batter into the lined springform pan and set in a cold oven. Turn to 350° F. and bake about 45 minutes or until the cake begins to pull away from the side of the pan.

5. Cool 20 minutes or until the top is barely warm. Turn the cake out onto a wire rack and remove the wax paper. Cool completely.

6. To make the icing: Place the chocolate and cream in a small bowl over barely simmering water. When the cream is hot enough to melt the chocolate, stir to blend thoroughly. Remove from the heat and whisk in the butter. Pour the icing over the cooled cake, smoothing it over and glazing the top and sides.

Makes 8 servings

TRANSPORTATION TIP

The iced cake can be lifted off the wire rack and placed on a plate for transportation and serving. It is moist enough that it shouldn't slide around. However, you might want to protect the top by enveloping the cake in a loose-fitting tent of aluminum foil. Or carry it in a cake holder especially designed for the task.

It's easiest to cut the cake on the spot, so don't forget cutting and serving utensils to do this.

If you don't want to take the entire cake, cut off individual pieces and wrap them separately. In this case, you might not want to ice the cake. Simply shake powdered sugar over the top of each serving at the site.

Peanut Butter and Banana Cake

If you're looking for a cake that travels well, this is it. Being as much like a quick bread as anything, the combination of peanut butter and banana melts into a tasty, friendly, sturdy blend. With additional peanut butter drizzled over the top, no one is likely to ask you what kind of cake this is.

Should you want to take it along on a breakfast outing, simply leave off the frosting and cut thin slices to sandwich around softened cream cheese.

Cake:
> *4 tablespoons unsalted butter*
> *3/4 cup chunky peanut butter*
> *1 cup light brown sugar*
> *3 eggs*
> *2 large bananas (1 cup mashed)*
> *2 cups all-purpose flour*
> *2 teaspoons baking soda*
> *1/4 teaspoon salt*

Icing:
> *1/4 cup chunky peanut butter*
> *1/3 cup light corn syrup*

1. To make the cake: Liberally grease an 8-cup Bundt pan. Dust the inside with flour and tap out any excess. Heat the oven to 325°F.

2. Place the butter and peanut butter in a mixing bowl and beat until well blended. Add the brown sugar and continue beating until the mixture is smooth and fluffy. Beat in the eggs one at a time, making sure the mixture thickens and becomes silky before adding another egg. Stir in the mashed bananas.

3. Stir together or sift the flour, baking soda, and salt to mix completely. Add this to the moist ingredients and stir until smooth. Pour into the prepared Bundt pan and smooth out the top. Bake for 55 to 60 minutes. Cool the cake in the pan for 10 minutes before turning it out onto a wire rack.

4. To make the icing: Stir together the peanut butter and corn syrup. It should be thin enough to fall from a spoon onto the cake but thick enough that it will hold its shape. Drizzle the icing over the top of the warm cake and allow it to finish cooling before cutting.

Makes 10 to 12 servings

TRANSPORTATION TIP

Transfer this cake to a serving plate before loosely covering with aluminum foil and packing. Or carry it in a special, enclosed cake holder. In either case, the cake does not need to be refrigerated or held in a cooler.

Cut it on site, remembering to bring the appropriate cutting and serving utensils.

Alternatively, the cake can be cut into individual pieces and wrapped in aluminum foil.

Rolled Lime Curd Cake with Raspberry Sauce

Nothing is more refreshing and elegant than this rolled lime sponge cake filled with lime curd custard and served with a smooth raspberry sauce.

Since it's rolled up—and without icing—this cake is particularly easy to pack up and carry about the countryside. Simply bring along a small dusting canister filled with confectioners' sugar and a container of the sauce. You can cut the cake and assemble the dessert on the spot.

Lime Curd Custard:

3/4 cup fresh lime juice (5 limes)
1 1/2 cups granulated sugar
3 eggs, beaten until frothy
3/4 cup unsalted butter, softened

Lime Sponge Cake:

4 eggs, separated
Pinch of salt
1/2 cup granulated sugar, divided
1 teaspoon fresh lime juice
1 teaspoon grated lime rind
3/4 cup cake flour
2 tablespoons confectioners' sugar

Raspberry Sauce:

1/2 pint fresh raspberries
2/3 cup granulated sugar
1 tablespoon framboise

1. To make the custard: Place the lime juice in a heavy-bottomed saucepan over medium-low heat. Gradually add the sugar and continue stirring until all the sugar is dissolved and no trace of graininess remains. Wipe down the sides of the pan with a brush or towel dipped in water.

2. Add the eggs and one-third of the butter and stir constantly until the butter is melted. Add the remaining butter in two stages, letting it melt each time. Continue stirring and cook over low heat until the mixture has thickened and reached 145° F. Only a drop or two of the custard should fall off the spoon when it is lifted out of the sauce. Be careful not to cook any further or the sauce will curdle.

3. Immediately transfer the custard to a bowl and stir occasionally as the mixture cools to prevent a skin from forming on the surface. Alternatively, place a piece of wax paper directly on the surface of the custard. Let it cool completely before starting the cake. The custard may be refrigerated.

4. To make the cake: Lightly grease a 15 1/2 X 10 1/2 X 1-inch jelly-roll pan and line with greased wax paper. Heat the oven to 375° F.

5. Place the egg whites in a round-bottomed metal bowl, add a pinch of salt, and beat just until the egg whites form a soft peak when the whisk is lifted out of the mixture. Whisk in 1/4 cup of the sugar, a tablespoon at a time, beating 10 seconds after each addition. After the sugar is added, continue beating until the whites hold a stiff peak.

6. Place the egg yolks in another bowl and gradually beat in the remaining 1/4 cup of sugar. Beat until the mixture is thick, pale yellow and falls from the whisk in a back-and-forth ribbon pattern. Stir in the lime juice.

7. Pour the beaten yolks over the egg whites and add the lime rind mixed with the cake flour. Gently fold everything together just until blended. Pour the batter into the prepared jelly-roll pan and spread it out to the edges.

8. Bake for 8 to 10 minutes, or until the cake springs back when lightly touched. Don't cook so long that the edges of the cake begin to harden. Cool the cake in the pan on a rack for 15 minutes.

9. Place a piece of wax paper on a work surface and dust it with confectioners' sugar. Turn the cake, upside down, onto the sugared wax paper. Remove the baking pan and peel off the wax paper liner that is now on top.

10. Spread the lime filling over the entire surface of the cake and then roll it up, starting at the short end. The cake should be pliable and easy to maneuver with the hands, though the wax paper may be used as a guide (just be careful not to roll it into the cake). When the cake is rolled all the way up, lift it off the paper, place it seam side down on a serving plate and refrigerate. When ready to use, dust the outside of the cake with confectioners' sugar.

11. To make the raspberry sauce: Place the raspberries and sugar in a blender or food processor and purée until smooth. Then strain the mixture into a bowl, discarding all the seeds that have been trapped by the sieve. Stir the framboise into the seedless sauce, cover, and refrigerate. Serve this on top or underneath slices of the cake.

Makes 8 to 10 servings

VARIATION

Strawberry Sauce

Substitute 1 pint of hulled strawberries for the raspberries. Substitute Cognac for framboise.

TRANSPORTATION TIP

This cake can travel with other cold foods in a cooler. If you don't have room, however, it will stay fine at room temperature for 3 or 4 hours. Cut and serve it at the site. If you only want to take a couple of pieces, however, these can be individually wrapped.

Store the chilled raspberry sauce in a separate, tightly covered dish or jar. For an elegant event, you might want to transfer the sauce to a special serving dish at the picnic.

Don't forget to bring along appropriate serving pieces and spoons.

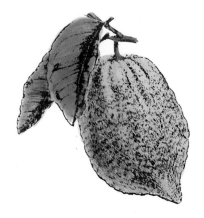

Peach and Cream Cheese Tart

This layered dessert is a nice juxtaposition of crisp and smooth. A sugar crust base is followed by a cream cheese filling, and the whole is topped with sliced peaches and a peach purée glaze. The rosy peach topping is especially appealing and refreshing on a hot summer afternoon.

Crust:

> 3 tablespoons unsalted butter, softened
> 1/3 cup granulated sugar
> 1/2 cup all-purpose flour
> 1/4 teaspoon salt

Filling:

> 4 ounces cream cheese
> 1 cup granulated sugar, divided
> 1 egg
> 1/2 teaspoon vanilla extract
> 3 cups peeled and thinly sliced fresh peaches,
>   divided (4 whole)
> 1/2 cup water
> 2 tablespoons cornstarch
> 2 teaspoons fresh lemon juice

1. To make the crust: Heat the oven to 400° F. Cream the butter and sugar in a mixing bowl, beating until the mixture is smooth and fluffy. Add the flour and salt and stir until the mixture begins to clump together. Scatter this in the base of a 9-inch springform pan and pack down, making a thin layer of crust. Bake for 7 or 8 minutes, just until the crust is set and begins to color at the edges. Cool on a wire rack and lower the oven temperature to 325° F.

2. To make the filling: Smear the cream cheese around a mixing bowl until it is smooth. Add 1/2 cup of the granulated sugar and beat until smooth and fluffy. Now beat in the egg and vanilla extract and mix until completely blended. Pour this mixture over the sugar crust and bake 20 minutes until the top has set and puffed up a little. Set aside to cool an a wire rack.

3. Place 1 1/2 cups of the peaches in a saucepan with the water and remaining 1/2 cup sugar. Bring to a boil over medium heat and cook until the peaches are soft. Stir constantly. Pass the peach mixture through a sieve or place in a blender or food processor and purée. Return this strained mixture to the saucepan, add the cornstarch, and bring to a boil for 1 minute. Off the heat, stir in the lemon juice.

4. Place the remaining 1 1/2 cups of peaches in concentric circles on top of the cream cheese filling. Pour the peach purée over this and place in the refrigerator to cool.

Makes 8 servings

TRANSPORTATION TIP

This tart travels to the picnic in the springform pan, covered with aluminum foil. It can be packed with other cold foods, though it will hold up for several hours without being chilled.

You may cut it in advance, removing the ring of the pan and then replacing it for transportation. You can also cut it on the spot, but be sure to bring a knife and serving wedge.

Apple Tart

Crisp, juicy Jonathans arriving at market are a harbinger of the fall to come. That's the time to put up apple butter and make apple cobblers. But for portability, this thin apple tart baked in a pizza pan can't be beat. The flaky crust and the brown sugar–glazed apples are an uncomplicated and light treat for weather that still has a chance of being sunny and warm.

Pastry:

2 cups all-purpose flour
1/2 cup chilled unsalted butter, cut into 1/4-inch
     cubes
1 teaspoon salt
3 tablespoons shortening
1/2 to 2/3 cup ice-cold water

Topping:

2 large Jonathan apples
1 tablespoon granulated sugar
1 tablespoon fresh lemon juice
1/4 cup, firmly packed, light brown sugar
1 tablespoon granulated sugar
1/2 teaspoon ground cinnamon

1. To make the pastry: Place the flour, cubes of cold butter, and salt in a large mixing bowl. Toss to coat the butter with flour. Then pinch and smear the butter between the fingertips to break it up into smaller pieces about the size of corn flakes or small peas. Now add the shortening and use a fork to break it up into similar-sized pieces. Slowly add about 1/2 cup of the water, tossing and mixing with a fork to moisten the flour. Continue adding water, a little at a time, until the mixture can be clumped together in a dough. Shape into a flattened round, wrap in wax paper, and refrigerate at least 30 minutes before rolling out.

2. To make the topping: While the pastry is in the refrigerator, quarter and core the apples but do not peel off the skin. Slice the apple sections lengthwise into paper-thin wedges. Place in a bowl and sprinkle with 1 table-spoon of granulated sugar and the lemon juice. Toss gently to mix everything and then let rest for 30 minutes to draw off some of the juice from the apples.

3. To finish the pastry: Heat the oven to 450° F. Dust both sides of the dough with flour and roll out into a 14-inch circle on a lightly floured, smooth work surface. Turn the dough occasionally, and dust with additional flour, if necessary, to prevent it from sticking. Gently fold the dough in half, and then in half again, being careful not to crease it. Then lift it into a 12-inch pizza pan and unfold and position the dough so it overlaps the sides of the pan slightly. Be careful, however, not to stretch it. Use the flat blade of a wide knife, sliding it across the rim of the pan, to scrape off excess dough. Prick the dough in eight or nine spots with the tines of a fork. Place in the heated oven and bake 10 to 12 minutes, until the crust has puffed up and set and is lightly browned all over. Cool on a wire rack and reduce the oven temperature to 425° F.

4. To finish the tart: Drain the apples and place them in three concentric circles around the baked pastry. Start about 1/2 inch from the outer edge and have the apples only barely overlapping. Mix together the light brown sugar, granulated sugar, and cinnamon. Scatter this mixture over the apples and bake about 15 minutes until the top is golden brown and the sugar is crusty and bubbly.

Makes 8 to 10 servings

TRANSPORTATION TIP

Take the tart to the picnic in the pizza pan loosely covered with aluminum foil. It doesn't require refrigeration or chilling in transit.

Cut it beforehand if you like—using a pizza wheel or a sharp knife. You can also slice it at the picnic. In that case, don't forget the knife and serving wedge.

Index

Afternoon menus, 46-55
Almond Fried Chicken, 78
Appetizers, 64-73
  butternut apple soup, 66
  carrot and leek soup, 67
  gravlax with sour cream mustard sauce, 70
  guacamole, 68
  ham and cheese puffs, 73
  marinated mushrooms, 69
  pimiento cheese, 71
  spinach puffs, 72
  tomato and cucumber soup, 65
  watercress and leek soup, 67
Apple Tart, 125
Apple-Glazed Pork Tenderloin, 75
Apples
  and butternut soup, 66
  pork tenderloin glazed with, 75
  tarts, 125
Asparagus in Lemon Sauce, 100

Baby Back Ribs with Barbecue Sauce, 76-77
Bacteria in food, 12, 13
Bagels, 42
Baked goods breakfast, 43
Bananas, and peanut butter cake, 121
Barbecue dinner, 59
Barbecue Sauce, 76-77
Barbecued Whole Pork Tenderloin, 75
Basil, dressing, and green beans, 95
Beach breakfast, 44
Beans, salad, 97
Beeton, Mrs. (author), 11
Beverages, Bloody Mary, 65
Block parties, 61
Bloody Mary, 65
Boating lunch, 50
Book of Household Management (Beeton), 11

Breads
  cinnamon-nut sandwich loaf, 111
  cornmeal muffins, 112
  cornmeal soda crackers, 114
  herb-cheese sandwich loaf, 110-11
  oatmeal spice muffins, 112
  pocketbook rolls, 109
  whole-wheat rolls, 113
Breakfast menus, 40-45
Butternut Apple Soup, 66

Caesar Pasta Salad with Tuna, 88
Cakes
  chocolate malted, 120
  lime curd with raspberry sauce, 122-23
  peanut butter and banana, 121
Candles, 30
Carrot and Leek Soup, 67
Carrots
  and leek soup, 67
  with zucchini and red onions, 99
Cheeses
  cream cheese and olive macaroni salad, 103
  cream cheese and peach tart, 124
  and ham puffs in phyllo, 73
  Jarlsberg and potato pie, 90-91
  pimiento, 71
  pullman sandwich loaf with, 110-11
  ricotta and onion pie, 89
Chewy Molasses Sugar Cookies, 117
Chicken
  almond fried, 78
  curried with grapes, 79
  as picnic staple, 12
  roasted, 80

Chili Molé, 81
China utensils, 26
Chocolate Malted Cake, 120
Chocolate motif at dinner, 60
Chocolate Raspberry Bars with Walnuts, 118
Cinnamon-Nut Sandwich Loaf, 111
Cold Tomato Sauce, 65
Cold Tomato Soup with Cucumber, 65
Cole Slaw, 94
Colorful dinner, 59
Containers, 15
Cookies, molasses sugar, 117
Coolers, 34
Cornmeal Muffins, 112
Cornmeal Soda Crackers, 114
Cream Cheese and Olive Macaroni Salad, 103
Creamy Corkscrew Pasta with Scallops and Vegetables, 87
Crystal, 27
Cucumber Soup, 84
Cucumbers
  in cold tomato soup, 65
  dilled tomatoes and, 98
  poached tuna in sauce of, 84
  soup, 84
Curried Chicken Salad with Grapes, 79

Deck dinner, 60
Decorations, 30
Desserts
  apple tarts, 125
  chocolate malted cake, 120
  chocolate raspberry bars with, 118
  lime curd cake, 122-23
  lime curd cake with raspberry sauce, 122-23
  molasses sugar cookies, 117
  peach and cream cheese tart, 124
  peanut butter and banana cake, 121

toffee bars, 119
Deviled Eggs, 93
Dilled Tomatoes and Cucumbers, 98
Dinners, 56-61
Dips, guacamole with pistachios, 68
Dressings
  basil, with green beans, 95
  honey, with fruit salad, 105
Drinks, Bloody Mary, 65

Easy lunch, 52
Eggs, deviled, 93
Entrées, 74-91
  almond fried chicken, 78
  baby back ribs, 76-77
  chili molé, 81
  curried chicken salad, 79
  flank steak Florentine, 82
  grilled lamb, 83
  Jarlsberg and potato pie, 90-91
  leg of lamb, 83
  onion and ricotta pie, 89
  pasta salad with tuna, 88
  pasta with scallops and vegetables, 87
  poached tuna, 84
  pork tenderloin, 75
  roasted chicken, 80
  salmon terrine, 86
  shrimp salad, 85
Evening menus, 56-61

Fish
  poached tuna with cucumber sauce, 84
  salmon (gravlax) with sour cream mustard sauce, 70
  salmon terrine with bay scallops, 86
  tuna with pasta salad, 88
  See also Shellfish
Flank Steak Florentine, 82
Foods
  convenience in transporting and serving of, 14-15
  keeping qualities of, 12-13

maintaining appropriate
temperatures of, 17
protection of, 21
wrapping of, 15
Football lunch, 51
Frozen foods, 13
Fruit Salad with Honey
Dressing, 105
Fruits
apple and butternut soup,
66
apple tarts, 125
apples and pork
tenderloin, 75
banana and peanut butter
cake, 121
grapes in curried chicken
salad, 79
lime curd cake, 122-23
peach and cream cheese
tart, 124
pineapple and raisins in
sweet potato salad, 106
raspberry and chocolate
bars, 118
raspberry sauce with lime
curd cake, 122-23
salad with honey
dressing, 105
strawberry sauce, 123

Garbage disposal, 36
Grapes, curried chicken
salad with, 79
Gravlax with Sour Cream
Mustard Sauce, 70
Green Beans with Basil
Dressing, 95
Grilled Baby Back Ribs, 76-77
Grilled Lamb on a Stick, 83
Grilled Leg of Lamb, 83
Grilling, on-site, 33
Ground covers, 29
Guacamole with Pistachios,
68

Ham and Cheese Puffs in
Phyllo, 73
Herb-Cheese Pullman
Sandwich Loaf, 110-11
Hiking breakfast, 44
Hiking lunch, 48, 50
Honey, dressing, with fruit
salad, 105

Insects, 21
Insulation for food, 13
International lunch, 53

Jarlsberg and Potato Pie,
90-91

Kids' lunch, 55

Lamb
grilled leg of, 83
grilled on stick, 83
Leeks
and carrot soup, 67
and watercress soup, 67
Lemon, sauce, with
asparagus, 100
Lighting, 30
Lime curd cake with
raspberry sauce, 122-23
Linens, 29
Lovers' meals
breakfast, 43
dinner, 58, 60
lunch, 52, 54
Lunches, 46-55

Mayonnaise, keeping
qualities of, 12
Meats
almond fried chicken, 78
apple-glazed pork
tenderloin, 75
baby back ribs with
barbecue sauce, 76-77
barbecued whole pork
tenderloin, 75
curried chicken salad
with grapes, 79
flank steak Florentine, 82
grilled baby back ribs,
76-77
grilled leg of lamb, 83
ham and cheese puffs, 73
lamb grilled on a stick, 83
pre-carving of, 15
roasted chicken, 80
Molasses sugar cookies, 117
Mushrooms, marinated, 69
Musical dinner, 61
Mustard and sour cream
sauce, gravlax in, 70

New Potato Salad, 102

Oatmeal Spice Muffins, 112
Olives, cream cheese and
macaroni salad with, 103
Onion and Ricotta Pie, 89
Onions
with carrots and zucchini,
99
and ricotta pie, 89

Packaging devices, 37
Paper utensils, 24
Park lunch, 49
Party dinner, 61
Pasta
cream cheese and olive
salad with, 103
salad with tuna, 88
with scallops and
vegetables, 87
Peach and Cream Cheese
Tart, 124
Peanut Butter and Banana
Cake, 121
Peppers
rice salad with, 104
salad, 96
Phyllo
ham and cheese puffs in,
73
spinach puffs in, 72
Picnic baskets, organization
of, 18-19
Picnic sets, 31
Pies
Jarlsberg and potato,
90-91
onion and ricotta, 89
Pimiento Cheese, 71
Pineapple, and raisins in
sweet potato salad, 106
Pistachios, guacamole with,
68
Plain Soda Crackers, 115
Plastic utensils, 24
Poached Tuna with
Cucumber Sauce, 84
Pocketbook Rolls, 109
Pork
baby back ribs, 75
ham and cheese puffs in
phyllo, 73
tenderloin, 75

Potatoes
and jarlsberg pie, 90-91
salad, 12, 102
Poultry
almond fried chicken, 78
curried chicken salad
with grapes, 79
roasted chicken, 80

Raisins, and pineapple in
sweet potato salad, 106
Raspberries
and chocolate bars, 118
sauce, 122-23
Raspberries and chocolate
bars with walnuts, 118
Ratatouille, 101
Red lunch, 55
Red Pepper Salad, 96
Red peppers
rice salad with, 104
salad, 96
Rice Salad with Red and
Yellow Peppers, 104
Ricotta, and onion pie, 89
Roasted Chicken, 80
Rolled Lime Curd Cake with
Raspberry Sauce, 122-23
Rolls, pocketbook, 109
Romantic meals
breakfast, 43
dinner, 58, 60
lunch, 52, 54
Rosy Marinated Mushrooms,
69

Sailing lunch, 48
Salads
bean, 97
chicken curried with
grapes, 79
cole slaw, 94
cream cheese and olive
macaroni, 103
fruit with honey dressing,
105
pasta with tuna, 88
potato, 102
red pepper, 96
rice with red and yellow
peppers, 104
shrimp, 85
sweet potato with pineapple
and raisins, 106

Salmon
  gravlax with sour cream
    mustard sauce, 70
  terrine with bay scallops,
    86
Salmon Terrine with Bay
  Scallops, 86
Salmonella poisoning, 12
Sauced Carrots, Zucchini,
  and Red Onions, 99
Sauces
  barbecue, 76-77
  cold tomato, 65
  lemon, with asparagus,
    100
  raspberry with rolled
    lime curd cake, 122-23
  sour cream mustard, 70
  strawberry, 123
Savory Bean Salad, 97
Scallops
  pasta and vegetables
    with, 87
  salmon terrine with, 86
Settings, 23-31
Shellfish
  bay scallops with salmon
    terrine, 86
  scallops and vegetables
    with pasta, 87
  shrimp salad, 85
Shrimp salad, 85
Side dishes, 92-107
  asparagus in lemon sauce,
    100
  bean salad, 97
  carrots, zucchini, and red
    onions, 99
  cole slaw, 94
  cream cheese and olive
    macaroni salad, 103
  deviled eggs, 93
  dilled tomatoes and
    cucumbers, 98
  fruit salad, 105
  green beans with basil
    dressing, 95
  potato salad, 102
  ratatouille, 101
  red pepper salad, 96
  rice salad with red and
    yellow peppers, 104

sweet potato salad, 106
Smorgasbord for breakfast,
  42
Soda crackers, 114-15
Soups
  butternut apple, 66
  carrot and leek, 67
  cold tomato with
    cucumber, 65
  cucumber, 84
  watercress and leek, 67
Sour cream and mustard
  sauce, gravlax in, 70
Spinach Puffs in Phyllo, 72
Staphylococcus aureus
  bacteria, 12
Steaks, Florentine flank, 82
Stews, ratatouille, 101
Strawberry Sauce, 123
Study in Red Shrimp Salad,
  85
Sunflower kernels,
  whole-wheat rolls with, 113
Sunlight, perishable foods
  and, 13
Sweet Potato Salad with
  Pineapple and Raisins,
  106

Thermoses, 34
Toffee Bars, 119
Tomato sauce, 65
Tomato soup, with
  cucumber, 65
Tomatoes, dilled with
  cucumbers, 98
Tuna
  pasta salad with, 88
  poached with cucumber
    sauce, 84

Up-scale dinner, 58
Utensils, 14-15
  china, 26
  cleanliness of, 13
  crystal, 27
  paper and plastic, 24

Vegetables
  asparagus in lemon sauce,
    100
  bean salad, 96
  dilled tomatoes and
    cucmbers, 98

green beans with basil
  dressing, 95
onion and ricotta pie, 89
pasta and scallops with, 87
peppers with rice salad,
  104
potato and Jarlsberg pie,
  90-91
potato salad, 102
ratatouille, 101
red pepper salad, 96
sauced carrots, zucchini,
  and red onions, 99
spinach puffs in phyllo,
  72
sweet potato salad with
  pineapples and raisins, 106

Walnuts, chocolate
  raspberry bars with, 118
Watercress and Leek Soup,
  67
Whole-Wheat Rolls with
  Sunflower Kernels, 113
Wrapping, 15

Yellow peppers, rice salad
  with, 104

Zucchini, with carrots and
  red onions, 99